REGULATING SPAM

A European Perspective after the
Adoption of the E-Privacy Directive

Series Editors

Aernout H.J. Schmidt, *Editor-in-Chief*
eLaw@Leiden, Centre for Law in the Information Society,
Leiden University

Philip E. van Tongeren, *Publishing Editor*
T · M · C · Asser press, The Hague

For other titles in the Series see p. 153

INFORMATION TECHNOLOGY & LAW SERIES ⑩

REGULATING SPAM

A European Perspective after the Adoption of the E-Privacy Directive

Lodewijk F. Asscher
Sjo Anne Hoogcarspel

T·M·C· ASSER PRESS

The Hague

The *Information Technology & Law Series* is published
by T·M·C·Asser press
P.O. Box 16163, 2500 BD The Hague, The Netherlands
<www.asserpress.nl>

T·M·C·Asser press English language books are distributed exclusively by:

Cambridge University Press, The Edinburgh Building, Shaftesbury Road,
Cambridge CB2 2RU, UK,
or
for customers in the USA, Canada and Mexico:
Cambridge University Press, 100 Brook Hill Drive, West Nyack, NY 10994-2133, USA

<www.cambridge.org>

The *Information Technology & Law Series* is an initiative of ITeR, the National Programme for
Information Technology and Law, which is a research programme set up by the Dutch
government and the Netherlands Organisation for Scientific Research (NWO) in The Hague.
Since 1995 ITeR has published all of its research results in its own book series. In 2002 ITeR
launched the present internationally orientated and English language *Information Technology
& Law Series*. This series deals with the implications of information technology for legal
systems and institutions. It is not restricted to publishing ITeR's research results. Hence,
authors are invited and encouraged to submit their manuscripts for inclusion. Manuscripts and
related correspondence can be sent to the Series' Editorial Office, which will also gladly
provide more information concerning editorial standards and procedures.

Editorial Office
eLaw@Leiden, Centre for Law in the Information Society
Leiden University
P.O. Box 9520
2300 RA Leiden, The Netherlands
Tel. +31(0)715277846
E-mail: <ital@law.leidenuniv.nl>
Web site: <www.nwo.nl/iter>

Single copies or Standing Order
The books in the *Information Technology & Law Series* can either be purchased as single
copies or through a standing order. For ordering information see the information on top of this
page or visit the publisher's web site at <www.asserpress.nl/cata/itlaw7/fra.htm>.

ISBN 10: 90-6704-220-X
ISBN 13: 978-90-6704-220-8
ISSN 1570-2782

Cover and lay-out: Oasis Productions, Nieuwerkerk a/d IJssel, The Netherlands

FOREWORD

The first draft of this study was the result of a research project carried out at the Institute for Information Law between September 2003 and March 2004. That report focused on the immediate question of implementation of the new Electronic Communications and Privacy directive. In 2005, miss Sjo Anne Hoogcarspel and I have worked on a thorough update of the report, adding more elaborate chapters on enforcement, international aspects of the fight against spam and national measures.

The Institute for Information Law (IViR) is part of the Faculty of Law of the University of Amsterdam. The Institute is the largest research facility in the field of information law in Europe. It employs over 25 qualified researchers who actively study and report on a wide range of subjects in the field of information law. The activities of the Institute include:

- research in the field of information law, initiated by the Institute or commissioned by third parties, including the European Commission, the WIPO and the Council of Europe;
- training of research assistants;
- organizing conferences and symposia;
- practical training (postgraduate courses, professional training, seminars);
- maintenance of a specialized library.

More information about IViR can be found at <www.ivir.nl>.

The initial idea of this research project followed from a round table conference, in May 2003. In spring, 2005, the editorial board of the IT&Law series invited us to work on a fuller study on the regulation of spam. This book aims to present an evaluation of recent legislative initiatives against Unsolicited Commercial E-mail (spam) in the European Union. It provides an analysis of the meaning and interpretation of the new regulatory regime for unsolicited communications within the EU. The book also addresses international aspects of the fight against spam, namely intra European activities and supra-national policies addressing spam. The book introduces some of the dilemmas of dealing with spam and the importance of effective enforcement mechanisms on that matter. The conclusions and recommendations aim to provide some directions, both in terms of further research as in terms of practical policy measures.

Amsterdam, October 2005   Lodewijk F. ASSCHER

TABLE OF CONTENTS

ABBREVIATIONS

BGBl.	Bundesgesetzblatt
CBP	College van Bescherming van Persoonsgegevens
CNIL	Commission Nationale de l'Informatique et des Libertés
CNSA	Contact Network of Spam Authorities
DPA	Data Protection Authorities
DPD	Data Protection Directive
EC	European Community
ECHR	European Convention on Human Rights
ECJ	European Court of Justice
EEA	European Economic Association
ETS	European Treaty Series
EU	European Union
FEDMA	Federation of European Direct Marketing
German LJ	German Law Journal
ICO	Information Commissioner's Office
ICT	Information and Communication Technologies
IP	Internet Protocol
ITU	International Telecommunication Union
IViR	Institute for Information Law
LAP	London Action Plan
MAPS	Mail Abuse Prevention System
MMS	Multi Media Messaging
MoU	Memorandums of Understanding

NJB	Nederlands Juristenblad
NJW	Neue Juristische Wochenschrift
NRA	National Regulatory Authorities
OECD	Organisation for Economic Co-operation and Development
OJ	Official Journal of the European Communities
OPTA	Onafhankelijke Post en Telecommunicatie Autoriteit
RBL	Realtime Blackhole List
SMS	Short Message Service
UBE	Unsolicited Bulk E-mail
UCE	Unsolicited Commercial E-mail
UPE	Unsolicited Pornographic E-mail
WIPO	World Intellectual Property Organisation
WSIS	World Summit on the Information Society

Chapter 1
REGULATING SPAM

Chapter 1
REGULATING SPAM

1.1 INTRODUCTION

This study analyses the legal framework regulating unsolicited commercial communications or spam in the European Union. Our focus is on the *Directive on privacy and electronic communications*[1] of 12 July 2002 (the E-Privacy Directive), as this directive has introduced new rules on the regulation of spam.

There are a number of reasons for conducting this study at this moment. First of all, the economic impact of spam is ever rising and so is the awareness of spam's cost to society.[2] Secondly and not coincidentally, the attention of the legislator towards spam came to a peak during the past four years, with the EU adopting its E-Privacy Directive, with its transposition deadline of 31 October 2003, and the US adopting their CAN SPAM Act 2003.[3] In 2004 and 2005 we have seen both the first results of the newly implemented legislation and a host of international initiatives to take the fight against spam a step further. It is fair to say that spam is also very much on the political agenda as lawmakers realize that junk e-mail has become a huge cost factor for businesses and a possible threat to consumer confidence.

This study is addressed to several related parties. Businesses must be aware of the legal changes and should use this report to focus on the practi-

---

[1] Directive 2002/58/EC of the European Parliament and of the Council of 12 July 2002 concerning the processing of personal data and the protection of privacy in the electronic communications sector (E-Privacy Directive).

[2] See Communication 2004, pp. 6-7.

[3] The Controlling the Assault of Non-Solicited Pornography and Marketing Act 2003, the CAN-SPAM Act, Pub.L. No. 108-187, 117 Stat. 2699 (2003), is a bill to regulate interstate commerce by imposing limitations and penalties on the transmission of unsolicited commercial electronic mail via the Internet.

L.F. Asscher and S.A. Hoogcarspel, Regulating Spam
© *2006, T·M·C·ASSER PRESS, The Hague, and the authors*

cal changes which will follow from the new legal environment. Consumers, on their part, should be aware of the real advantages of the new Directive but also of its inherent restrictions. Lawmakers may find it useful to have a brief overview of legislative initiatives as well as some critical notions on the effectiveness of the regulation of spam.

On a more general level, attempts to regulate spam pose questions that are very interesting for a number of reasons. First, the proliferation of spam in publicly available networks puts some communications law principles in a whole new light. For example, one of the classical ground rules used to be the obligation to transport all mail offered to the postal service provider indiscriminately.[4] The twin principle of communications secrecy and the obligation to carry for a common carrier have evolved into an almost dogmatic aspect of the relevant field of law. Now that most or all of the communication service providers consist of private parties and now that their networks are overflowed with unsolicited e-mails, it is fair to take a new look at old principles. Also, as everybody concedes that the solution to spam is to be found in a combination of technology and law, the problem of how to cope with spam might shed light on the future development of the interaction between law and information technology. The fact that law and technology are intertwined and that law and information technology look at each other to provide answers is in a way symbolic of a lot of other problems of tech regulation.

Our main research objective is to assess the practical legal consequences of the new regulatory regime. The question we therefore have to answer is: What are the consequences of the new regulatory regime of unsolicited communications, as introduced in (Art. 13 of) the new E-Privacy Directive?

Main research question:

How does the new regulatory regime change Spam law within the EU?

To answer that question we have to answer a number of sub-questions. First of all, we need to compare the new regime with the legal landscape before

---

[4] See for example De Sola Pool 1983, chapter 5.

the E-Privacy Directive. This requires us to assess the other relevant European Directives as well as related initiatives. Secondly, if we want to be able to say something about the consequences that the Directive will have, we will need to find out what the Directive does *not* regulate. In other words, we will have to find the gray areas or weak spots in the new regulation. We will also take a look at the definitions used in the Directive.

What does it say about virus-spam? And how about Spim? Are popup messages covered? And who is addressed by this new regime and who is protected by Article 13? Related but different is the question as to what margin of regulation is left to Member States. It is a question of EU law whether any room is left for national interpretation or national choices to be made in implementing new European legislation. Therefore we will have to map the space left for national choices. In order to make a valuable assessment of the new regime we will have to take a close look at the wording, exceptions and history of the main article of material law, Article 13. This implies an analysis of the meaning of Article 13's sections and their relation to other parts of the new regulatory framework. Article 13's relation with other sections of the E-Privacy Directive will subsequently be addressed. In order to evaluate the practical consequences, the next question we will have to answer is what new obligations the Directive has created for Member States, businesses and consumers and what consequences that has for liability issues. Important in this respect is the way Member States implemented the E-Privacy Directive into their national laws. Also, while our main focus will be on EU law, because for a practical solution to the spam problem, international co-operation with third countries is crucial, we cannot ignore the supra European dimensions of the spam phenomenon. This should lead to a concise answer to our main research question and to a number of conclusions and recommendations.

Sub questions:

- How should spam be defined
- What is the meaning of Article 13 of the E-Privacy Directive?
- What is the meaning of other articles of the E-Privacy Directive?
- Is e-mail address harvesting legal?
- What margin of appreciation is left to Member States?

- In what way did Member States implement the Directive?
- How is the new law enforced?
- In what way do countries co-operate to fight spam effectively?
- What alternatives are there to Article 13?

The question we strive to answer in this study touches several fields of law. Therefore this study cannot only focus on telecommunications law but also has to take into account some European constitutional law aspects. Also, in order to make a qualified assessment of the liabilities or obligations created we touch on aspects of civil law. Finally, regulating spam raises several fundamental rights issues. When we look at the harvesting of e-mail addresses by spammers, important questions of data protection law arise. Not only is spam regulated in a directive harmonizing *privacy* law, but prohibiting spam also has implications for freedom of *speech*,[5] whereas ISP monitoring of e-mail traffic might mean restricting the right to *confidentiality* of communications. Apart from a legal problem, spam is very much a technical problem. We do point out the interaction between technical and legal solutions at some points throughout this report. Our focus however remains on the legal aspects of the regulation of spam.

Relevant fields of law:

- Telecommunications Law
- EU constitutional law
- Fundamental rights law
- Data protection law
- Civil tort/liability law

We have chosen to leave several aspects of spam regulation out of our research plan.

We do not strive to present the full regulatory framework on the regulation of electronic communications in this study. We focus solely on the regulation of unsolicited communications which means that we do not pay attention to general questions of telecom regulation as for example the debate on the exact scope of a 'Publicly available Network' or the future posi-

---

[5] On spamming and free speech, see, *inter alia*, Geisler 2001.

tion of National Regulatory Authorities. This study does not strive to present an updated evaluation of the technological solutions to spam or a 'how to' manual on preventing spam from entering the reader's mailbox. In our concluding chapter we will pay attention to the complementing factors of technological solutions to spam and consumer awareness issues but the focus of this study remains on legal questions.

> **Outside the scope of our study:**
>
> - General Framework on electronic communications
> - Technological aspects
> - Economical Analysis
> - How-to manual

The contents of this report are as follows. This first chapter will introduce the spam problem and will take a look at current definitions of spam and the parties involved as well as past spam regulation. In chapter 2, we will analyze Article 13 of the E-Privacy Directive. Chapter 3 deals spam and security, whereas chapter 4 analyses the problem of e-mail address harvesting. Chapter 5 covers issues of implementation and enforcement, followed by a chapter on international co-operation and challenges to effective cross-border enforcement. Chapter 7 touches upon other aspects of the fight against spam. Chapter 8 then contains our conclusions and recommendations.

In our final chapter, an overall analysis of the consequences of the new regulatory regime is presented. Focus will be on practical legal consequences for consumers, businesses and governments. Recommendations will be presented as to where legal uncertainties should be cleared up and what the role of national governments can be in that process. Finally, in the annexed management summary a checklist of relevant legal questions to be used by businesses after implementation of the Directive is presented.

1.2 SPAM: INTRODUCING THE LEGAL PROBLEM

The term spam, a trademark for canned ham by the firm Hormel, is said to be derived from a Monty Python sketch which took place in a restaurant, in

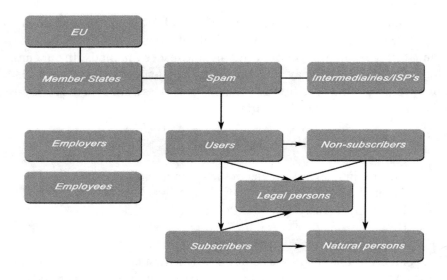

which canned ham was present on the menu. Somewhere in the mid-1980's the word spam was posted repeatedly on Usenet, causing technical difficulties. Such postings became known as 'spamming'. Gradually, since the beginning of the 1990's, the term spam became commonly used to describe unwanted e-mail, often consisting of advertisements for products and services of a dubious nature.[6] Even though the term spam is associated with unsolicited e-mail, it could also be used to describe all unwanted messages such as voice-mail, fax and possibly other media. Spam however is not an official notion as such.

Spam affects many interested and interrelated parties. As a result, different viewpoints exist with respect to the problems relating to spam. These are the perspectives of users of communications services such as the internet, intermediaries and of course the State. Users can be divided into: subscribers and non-subscribers, natural and legal persons, recipients and spammers. Intermediaries can be internet service providers or network service providers, or both. Finally, the State has to implement the rules of this Directive. All of these parties have obligations, and obligations may imply liability. Another category consists of vendors, the corporations that hire spammers

---

[6] Magee 2003, p. 3.

to exercise spam runs on their behalf. We will examine the possibilities to hold them liable as well.

1.3   DEFINING SPAM

The problem of spam can be viewed from different angles. First, spam poses an economic problem, shifting the burden of the cost of advertisement from the advertiser to the recipient as well as to the companies that are transporting the advertisement. From another point of view spam is also a human rights issue, with conflicting interests regarding freedom of speech and the right to privacy.

To put spam in a definition proves rather difficult. There is no global consensus on a definition of spam.[7] Various definitions of spam have surfaced over the years. The best known short definitions are Unsolicited Bulk E-mail (UBE) and Unsolicited Commercial E-mail (UCE), but also Unsolicited Commercial Bulk E-mail and just Unsolicited Electronic Mail have been used.[8] In its 2004 Communication the European Commission aptly notes that: '"Spam" is a term more often used than defined. In short, it is commonly used to describe unsolicited, often bulk e-mails. [...] ... the concept of "spam" is used in this Communication as a shortcut for unsolicited commercial electronic mail.'[9] Most definitions of spam contain the following elements: unsolicited, bulk, commercial.[10] Two recurring combinations in the literature on spam are: UCE (unsolicited commercial e-mail) and UBE (unsolicited bulk e-mail). This invokes questions as: can non-com-

---

[7] Report of the Working Group on Internet Governance 2005, p. 6.

[8] Sorkin 2000, p. 328.

[9] Communication 2004, p. 5.

[10] The US CAN-SPAM Act regulates 'commercial electronic mail' and does not specifically mention 'unsolicited' as a defining element. Therefore, the provisions of the CAN-SPAM Act also apply to commercial electronic mail that is solicited. According to the statute, an e-mail will constitute CAN-SPAM Act spam, when it falls within the definition of 'commercial electronic mail' and if it fails to comply with any of the other relevant provisions within the statute. The CAN-SPAM Act defines 'commercial electronic mail' as being: 'any electronic mail message the primary purpose of which is the commercial advertisement or promotion of a commercial product or service' (S. 3 (2)(A)) The Act does not seek to prohibit the nuisance the spam creates; rather it intends to prohibit e-mail behaviour that is fraudulent, deceptive or otherwise misleading. Fritzemeyer & Law 2005, pp. 82-83.

mercial unsolicited e-mail be spam? Can a single e-mail be spam? The E-Privacy Directive does not give a definition of spam. The Directive refers to unsolicited communications for direct marketing purposes (recital 40). This report will not focus on finding the ultimate definition of spam either. However, the so-called utopian definition of spam springs to mind: 'All e-mails which are of no benefit to the recipient from the point of view of the recipient.'[11]

'Unsolicited' seems to be the keyword of any method to describe, to prevent and to fight spam. The elements 'bulk' and 'commercial' only gain meaning in relation to the unsolicited nature of the message. The use of bulk as a defining element seems to be blind to content relates to the problems caused by the massive amounts of spam being sent. That element poses the question of whether one single e-mail can be spam. To a particular user it does not matter if and how many others receive the same message. Also, a user does not want to have to find out whether other users have received the same message, before action can be taken. And how many people must receive a message before a spam run is considered to fulfill the notion of bulk? A fixed threshold would be circumvented by spammers and legitimize all spam runs beneath that level.[12] The lack of a definition of spam in the E-Privacy Directive points to an approach based on the principle of permission, not quantity, as Recital 40 of the E-Privacy Directive seems to imply.

Using the notion 'commercial' as a manner to distinguish spam from other unsolicited communications poses several problems. The E-Privacy Directive uses the notion 'direct marketing', a notion which contains other difficulties, as we will see in chapter 4. What are the questions raised by the use of the notion 'commercial' as a distinguishing element?

First, different jurisdictions use different interpretations of the notion commercial. For instance, are semi-privatized 'public' services as education and health care, for which a fee is paid, commercial?[13] National legislation has to clarify what belongs in this category and what does not. Secondly, it is to be considered whether a political statement can also be considered a commercial message. A Dutch Court labeled a spam run on

---

[11] Khong 2000, p. 3.
[12] Sorkin 2000, p. 333.
[13] Khong 2000, p. 2.

Members of Parliament as 'commercial' since the company behind the spam run had a financial interest in influencing the opinion of the Members of Parliament and their votes.[14] The latter criterion would render e-mails without a direct offer or adversarial content commercial. Thirdly, it is to be seen whether a request for a donation by a non-profit organization is to be considered a commercial message. In our opinion *non-profit* does not necessarily mean that a professional charity organization does not have any financial interests. Most professional non-profit organizations have a paid staff alongside volunteers. Employees have to be paid; therefore there is a 'commercial' interest to stay in business.

There is a danger in trying to define spam by content, apart from the above-mentioned risks of censorship and breach of confidentiality of communication. The burden of spam is not defined by the commercial nature of it *per se*. People can be annoyed by non-commercial messages just as well. And intermediaries suffer from the overload of spam, irrespective of content.[15]

A new and emerging problem is created by convergence of spam and computer viruses. In some cases, viruses seem to be used to distribute spam through the computer facilities of unknowing users, thus turning spam into a security threat in its own right.[16] This poses the question whether messages that are distributed by means of a virus fit the (or a) definition of spam. Those messages are unsolicited, sent in bulk and they might have a commercial element, for instance if the virus strikes out a competitive software system, or results in an attack of the web site of a competitor (Denial of Service attack). And to reverse the question, whether spam can be a

---

[14] *Staat* v. *Rath*, Court Almelo, 13 September 2000, *Mediaforum* 2002-11/12, pp. 366-370, with a comment by Catrien Noorda.

[15] Bergfeld & Lodder 2002, pp. 1051-1052.

[16] E.g., the 1999 Melissa virus; Sorkin 2002, p. 336. According to the MessageLabs Intelligence report 2005, in June 2005, the global ratio of e-mail-borne viruses to e-mail from new and unknown bad sources, for which the recipient addresses were deemed valid, was 1 in 28.2 (3.6%). In this report, MessageLabs notes that the motivation behind the latest e-mail borne threats is different than traditional methods of large scale attacks. No longer is the threat simply one of being caught up in collateral virus damage targeting the on-line world at large, or to hijack machines to send spam, but new criminal methods show a preference for selecting a particular target, whether an individual or an organization. Often such attacks are financially, competitively, politically or socially motivated. The attackers for example are seeking to steal confidential corporate information or intellectual intelligence.

security risk is also relevant for the legal prohibition of sending out spam. Does a spammer have to act deliberately?[17] Is there a duty to make sure your machine is secure? It is also important to know whether a user that does not use firewall or anti-virus software can as a result of this be held liable for spam runs sent from his computer (without his knowledge). New developments in which spam and viruses will grow into new shapes of nuisance will necessarily result in new legal questions. At this point it suffices to conclude that in this study we will follow the approach taken by the E-Privacy Directive on what is spam, i.e., we will use 'unsolicited communications for direct marketing purposes' as our general definition.

1.4   SPAM: THE ECONOMICS

If one looks at the economic consequences of spam, it is obvious that spam is a very cheap medium for marketing all kinds of goods and services.[18] Telemarketing in general has become increasingly popular as a direct marketing strategy. Direct marketing is an important tool to approach customers. E-mail may well be the cheapest vehicle for direct marketing; costs do not vary according to distance and repeated e-mails have very low additional costs. The more e-mails a spammer can send, the greater the profit, while costs remain nearly constant.[19] In sum, e-mail marketing can be very cheap. That is, cheap for the advertiser. The cost of sending out one million e-mails is minimal compared to the cost of obtaining a comparable level of exposure through paper advertisements or television commercials. The main reason for this imbalance is that part of the costs is imposed on other parties, namely the transporting intermediaries and the recipients. This is called cost-shifting.

Users of communication services have to pay to download the advertisement to their mailboxes, either through dial-up time or through an all-in package, the size of which has to be increased with the amount of e-mail and consequently the amount of bits the user receives. Apart from these costs, every minute spent on deleting spam is a waste of time, and therefore

---

[17] Bergfeld & Lodder 2002, pp. 1051-1052.
[18] Gauthronet & Drouard 2001, p. 2.
[19] OECD 2004.

Forecast Spam Messages Sent (Billions)

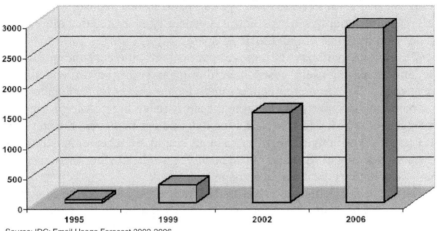

Source: IDC; Email Usage Forecast 2002-2006

money. The intermediaries transporting the message also pay for the cost of spam. They need to increase their bandwidth and server storage capacity to keep up with the increase of e-mail traffic. These costs are eventually compensated by higher fees for their services. The recipients are therefore paying more for their access subscription.[20] Free e-mail services might disappear.[21] The internet gets more expensive for its users, and therefore becomes a less accessible medium than it originally was.

Finally, apart from recipients and intermediaries who directly pay the costs of spam, another paying party is comprised of bona fide companies that do not send unsolicited e-mails.[22] Their solicited messages disappear into the enormous amount of unsolicited advertisements. Their image as an advertiser is compromised by advertisements which are annoying recipients through costs and content. The use of illegal spam runs by some companies as a means to advertise their products or service gives them an unfair competitive advantage. Getting rid of spam would be of benefit to the so-

---

[20] Sorkin 2000, pp. 336-337.

[21] Magee 2003, p. 4.

[22] As was the point of view of several committees during the discussion of the proposal of the E-Privacy Directive, see Magee 2003, p. 17.

called permission marketers. An opt-in regime would add to the promotion of European e-commerce. In recent years, spam has reached worrying numbers. Despite variations in statistics, it is generally estimated that more than 60 per cent of global e-mail traffic is 'spam'.

Cleaning up mailboxes to remove spam is both time consuming for the user and increasing users' costs when filtering and other software facilities are needed.[23] Furthermore, spam creates considerable costs for businesses.

Spam can also prompt liability for the entity receiving it. A company, for instance, could be held liable for failing to take steps to prevent the creation of a hostile work environment in case an employee receives unsolicited pornographic e-mail. But also 'false positives' – blacklisting the wrong e-mail – can create considerable damage.

The European Commission has stated that it is very difficult to calculate the total cost of spam. Nevertheless, it is clear that the total damage is a multi-billion Euro matter. Apart from that, the Commission is also and rightfully worried about the consequences of spam for consumer confidence in e-commerce and the Information Society.[24]

1.5   SPAM AND FUNDAMENTAL RIGHTS

Spam is also a fundamental rights problem. From the viewpoint of individuals, spam can be deemed an invasion of privacy. From the viewpoint of a spammer, quite often freedom of speech is involved. The most important fundamental rights involved in regulating spam are therefore freedom of expression and privacy. These fundamental rights apply to recipients as well as spammers and their clients. The fundamental rights in question are relevant with respect to state legislation and enforcement thereof, i.e., the

---

[23] Communication 2004, pp. 6-7. Do people care? Perhaps, the number of complaints is an indication. According to the 2004 Communication, the French SpamBox had attracted 325.000 messages in three months. A similar experience in Belgium led to 50.000 complaints in 2.5 months. Communication 2004, p. 7. In the Netherlands, from May 2004 till May 2005, 7114 complaints were filed at a web site specifically designed for this purpose, <www.spamklacht.nl>. Press release, 'Resultaten eerste jaar spambestrijding positief', 3 June 2005, <www.opta.nl>. For more on the filing of complaints about spam in different Member States, chapter 5.4.3.

[24] Communication 2004, p. 8.

Spam Triangle

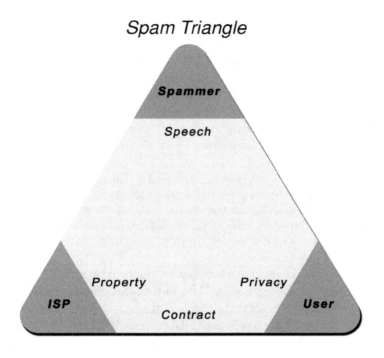

vertical application of fundamental rights. Fundamental rights can also have effect between private parties; this is called the horizontal application of fundamental rights. This may be the case with regard to the relation between recipients and spammers and their clients, but also between recipients and spammers on one side and intermediaries that filter e-mail on the other. The fundamental rights issues with regard to spam because of the triangular relation between user, spammer and ISP.

The spam triangle: the spammer will claim he is using his right to freedom of expression. The user sees his privacy interfered with. Both relational privacy in terms of filling his mailbox without his consent and informational privacy because his e-mail address is being used and processed without his consent. The provider has a contractual relationship with both the spammer and the user and can under certain circumstances claim property rights in his network. On the other hand, the user may have a contractual claim against the provider to get his e-mail without spam. Therefore, a number of rights collisions are part of the spam problem.

The right to freedom of expression is, *inter alia*, protected by Article 10 of the European Convention on Human Rights (ECHR).[25] The right to freedom of expression is not restricted to individuals. In principle, legal persons enjoy freedom of expression too. Apart from corporations, also charity organizations and political parties make use of direct e-marketing. Political statements are more strongly protected under the flag of freedom of expression than commercial messages. As the European Commission of Human Rights put it in the Scientology case:

> 'Although the Commission is not of the opinion that commercial "speech" as such is outside the protection conferred by Article 10(1), it considers that the level of protection must be less than that accorded to the expression of 'political' ideas, in the broadest sense, with which the values underpinning the concept of freedom of expression in the Convention chiefly are concerned.'[26]

Businesses have the right to market their products through advertisements. They enjoy freedom of expression. The European Court of Human Rights has acknowledged this in several cases over the past 25 years.[27] As a consequence, the test of Article 10(2) is available and obligatory for the assessment of the admissibility of national restrictions on commercial advertising. This test provides for legal examination of the clarity and the accessibility of the relevant limitation; the legitimacy of its aims and the important question of whether the limitation or prohibition is necessary in a democratic

---

[25] European Convention on Human Rights, Rome, 4 November 1950. Text completed by Protocol No. 2 (*ETS* No. 44) of 6 May 1963 and amended by Protocol No. 3 (*ETS* No. 45) of 6 May 1963, Protocol No. 5 (*ETS* No. 55) of 20 January 1966 and Protocol No. 8 (*ETS* No. 118) of 19 March 1985.

[26] *Yearbook of the European Convention of Human Rights*, 1979, p. 252.

[27] *X and Church of Scientology* v. *Sweden*, Appn. No. 7805/77, Decision on admissibility by the European Commission of Human Rights of 5 May 1979, DR 16, p. 68; *Jacubowski* v. *Germany*, Judgment of the European Court of Human Rights of 23 June 1994, *Series A*, No. 219; *Casado Coca* v. *Spain*, Judgment of the European Court of Human Rights of 24 February 1994, *Series A*, No. 285; *Markt Intern Verlag GmbH & Klaus Beermann* v. *Germany*, Judgment of the European Court of Human Rights of 20 November 1989, *Series A*, No. 165; *Hempfing* v. *Germany*, Appn. No. 14622/89, Decision on admissibility by the European Commission of Human Rights of 7 March 1991, DR 69, p. 272; *Barthold* v. *Germany*, Judgment of the European Court of Human Rights of 25 March 1985, *Series A*, No. 90; *Stambuk* v. *Germany*, Appn. No. 37928/97, Judgment of the European Court of Human Rights of 17 October 2002.

society, i.e., an examination of whether the national rule is appropriate and proportionate to its aim. However, the European Court of Human Rights applies a broad margin of appreciation when assessing the admissibility of national content-restrictions on commercial advertising.[28] This means that national authorities have a rather great freedom in their policy with regard to restrictions on the content of advertising.[29] The right to freedom of expression can therefore be restricted with regard to content, e.g., to protect the public in moral and health issues. Spam containing pornographic images can be perceived as offensive.[30] Spam promoting Viagra without warning of the possible consequences for heart patients can for example be seen as a health hazard.[31] The right to freedom of expression can also be restricted to protect the rights of others, such as the right to privacy.

The right to privacy, as protected by Article 8 ECHR, can conceptually be divided in informational privacy, privacy of communications and relational privacy.[32] In short, informational privacy is the individual's right to decide which personal data can be communicated to others. In chapter 4, we will discuss whether electronic mail addresses can be considered personal data. Processing of such data, which includes the collection, storage or use of electronic addresses could intrude on this informational privacy right. Privacy of communications or confidentiality of communications can be relevant with regard to filtering of e-mail.

Relational privacy includes the right to determine which communications one wishes to receive or not.[33] Freedom of expression and the right to be left alone can obviously conflict. The spam issue therefore reflects a conflict between freedom of expression and the right to privacy. The State has to balance both interests in the process of drawing up national legislation.

The clash between the freedom of expression of the spammer and the right to privacy of the person who does not want to receive spam is evident.

---

[28] Compare on the 'right to antenna', *Verein gegen Tierfabriken* v *Switzerland,* Appn. No. 24699/94, Judgment of the European Court of Human Rights of 28 June 2001.

[29] Kabel 2003b, pp. 4-5.

[30] Sorkin 2001, p. 336.

[31] See Kabel 2000, p. 9 on prescription of drugs and medical advice on the internet.

[32] Kabel 2003a, p. 6.

[33] Kabel 2003a, p. 6.

Service providers who have to service both groups of users are caught in the middle. They themselves suffer from an overload of spam which requires expansion of capacity of both technical assets and human resources. To target outbound spam, service providers include anti-spam provisions in their standard license agreements and close down accounts if their anti-spam policy is ignored. These procedures should be applied carefully because they could themselves encroach upon freedom of expression.

To prevent spam from entering their mail servers (and sometimes even from leaving them) service providers use filtering. Filtering can also infringe on fundamental rights such as freedom of expression and privacy. Use of filters and blocking of servers can restrict people's ability to communicate and therefore be an impairment of freedom of speech. This applies to spammers as well as to people who would actually like to receive spam, be it for pleasure or business. Blocking all spam by technical means without the e-mail user's consent could therefore intrude on the right to receive (and send) information, including spam messages. Filtering can also result in blocking legitimate information, the so-called false positives. This can be an infringement of the right to freedom of expression, even of persons who do not spam at all.

The E-Privacy Directive strikes a balance between freedom of speech and the right to privacy and property rights. This point of view is reflected by Recital 40 of the E-Privacy Directive which mentions both the invasion of privacy and the cost-shifting argument, in relation to receiving and transmitting parties, as a ground to impose an opt-in regime.

Recital 40 E-Privacy Directive

Safeguards should be provided for subscribers against intrusion of their privacy by unsolicited communications for direct marketing purposes in particular by means of automated calling machines, faxes, and e-mails, including SMS messages. These forms of unsolicited commercial communications may on the one hand be relatively easy and cheap to send and on the other may impose a burden and/or cost on the recipient. Moreover, in some cases their volume may also cause difficulties for electronic communications networks and terminal equipment. For such forms of unsolicited communications for direct marketing, it is justified to

require that prior explicit consent of the recipients is obtained before such communications are addressed to them. The single
market requires a harmonized approach to ensure simple, Com-
munity-wide rules for businesses and users.

1.6   OLD LEGAL FRAMEWORK

Now that we have discussed how spam is defined, we will take a look at the
regulation of spam before the E-Privacy Directive. In this section, European Directives which address(ed) unsolicited communications are presented
in chronological order. They show the enigmatic history of European regulation of unsolicited communications. The new framework for electronic
communications and the E-Privacy Directive will be discussed later on.

1.6.1   Data Protection Directive

The 1995 Data Protection Directive[34] provides general rules for the processing of personal data. Personal data are data which allow for identification of an individual. The Data Protection Directive does not target spam in
particular. However, e-mail addresses can be personal data.[35] The Article
29 Working Party, the advisory committee of European Data Protection
Authorities, declared in 2000 the harvesting of e-mail addresses on the
internet as amounting to unlawful processing of personal data according to
the rules of the Data Protection Directive.[36]

   According to Recital 10 and Article 1(2) of the E-Privacy Directive, the
general regime on data processing of the Data Protection Directive applies

---

[34] Directive 95/46/EC of the European Parliament and of the Council of 24 October
1995 on the protection of individuals with regard to the processing of personal data and on
the free movement of such data, *OJ* L 281, 23.11.1995, p. 31.
   [35] Schaub 2002, p. 4.
   [36] Art. 29 Working Party 2000a. The Art. 29 Working Party was set-up pursuant to Art.
29 of Directive 95/46/EC. It is an independent European advisory body on the protection of
data and privacy. Its missions are laid down in Art. 30 of Directive 95/46/EC and in Art. 14
of Directive 97/66/EC, <http://europa.eu.int/comm/privacy>. Documents of the Working
Party can be found on: <http://europa.eu.int/comm/internal_market/en/dataprot/wpdocs/
index.htm>.

alongside the special regime on electronic communications of the E-Privacy Directive. In chapter 4 we will explain which electronic addresses can be classified as personal data and which rules of both Directives therefore apply.

1.6.2   Distance Selling Directive

The 1997 Distance Selling Directive[37] is the first Directive to protect consumers from unsolicited communications. The Directive requires prior consent of the consumer for the use of automated calling systems without human intervention (automatic calling machine) and fax as a means of distance communication for the conclusion of a contract between consumer and supplier (Art. 10 (1)). According to Article 10(2), other means of distance communication which allow individual communications, may be used only where there is no clear objection from the consumer. The first provision refers to an opt-in regime for automatic calling machines and faxes. The technology neutral formula of the second provision seems to imply an opt-out regime for other unsolicited communications, including unsolicited e-mail.[38]

1.6.3   Telecommunications Privacy Directive (ISDN Directive)

The 1997 ISDN Directive[39] contained provisions on unsolicited calls. Article 12 prescribed an opt-in regime for the use for purposes of direct marketing of automated calling machines without human intervention, including fax machines (provision 1). Unsolicited calls for purposes of direct marketing by other means could be governed by either an opt-in or an opt-out regime, depending on the choice of individual Member States (provision 2). Some countries interpreted e-mail as falling into the category of 'calls by other means'.[40] The Article 29 Working Party is of the opinion that:

---

[37] Directive 97/7/EC of the European Parliament and of the Council of 20 May 1997 on the Protection of Consumers in respect of Distance Contracts *OJ* L 144, 4.6.1999, p. 19.

[38] Schaub 2002, p. 5.

[39] Directive 97/66/EC of the European Parliament and of the Council of 15 December 1997 concerning the processing of personal data and the protection of privacy in the telecommunications sector (incl. Annex), *OJ* L 24, 30.01.1998, p. 1.

[40] Magee 2003, p. 20.

'the telecommunication legal framework should apply to Internet services in the same way as it applies to other forms of communication...processing of personal data on the Internet has to respect data protection principles just as in the off-line world. Personal data processing on the Internet therefore has to be considered in the light of both data protection directives.'[41]

The European Commission subsequently issued a proposal for a new Directive. The Telecommunications Privacy Directive has now been replaced by the E-Privacy Directive.

1.6.4 E-Commerce Directive

The 2000 Directive on Electronic Commerce (E-Commerce Directive)[42] is the first Directive to explicitly mention electronic mail as an example of unsolicited communication in its recital.

> **Recital 30 E-Commerce Directive**
>
> The sending of unsolicited commercial communications by electronic mail may be undesirable for consumers and information society service providers and may disrupt the smooth functioning of interactive networks; the question of consent by recipient of certain forms of unsolicited commercial communications is not addressed by this Directive, but has already been addressed, in particular, by Directive 97/7/EC and by Directive 97/66/EC; in Member States which authorize unsolicited commercial communications by electronic mail, the setting up of appropriate industry filtering initiatives should be encouraged and facilitated; in addition it is necessary that in any event unsolicited commercial communities are clearly identifiable as such in order to improve transparency and to facilitate the functioning of such industry initiatives; unsolicited commercial communications by electronic

---

[41] Art. 29 Working Party 2000b, p. 3.

[42] Directive 2000/31/EC of the European Parliament and of the Council of 8 June 2000 on certain legal aspects of information society services, in particular electronic commerce, in the Internal Market ('Directive on electronic commerce'), *OJ* L 178, 17.07.2000, p. 1.

> mail should not result in additional communication costs for the recipient.

The Directive also contains specific provisions to protect users from unsolicited commercial communications by electronic mail. Article 7(1) states that when commercial communications are permitted by Member States, these communications shall be identifiable clearly and unambiguously upon receipt of the message. This means that the header of the message must contain a label like 'ADV' (advertisement) so the receiving party does not have to open the mail to be aware of its commercial content. Article 7(2) imposes an obligation to consult and respect opt-out registers regarding unsolicited commercial communications by electronic mail.

This has been interpreted as the Directive leaving Member States the choice between opt-in and opt-out regimes, although Recital 30 of the E-Commerce Directive specifically states that the question of consent is not addressed by this Directive.[43]

During the preparation of the E-Privacy Directive opinions were put forward against regulating spam in a separate Directive with an opt-in regime because Article 7 of the E-Commerce Directive and the General Data Protection Directive would already make regulation of electronic mail by Member States possible. Arguments were: regulatory inefficiency, penalizing responsible marketers and hindering the development of e-commerce within the EU, reducing the impetus for business to develop effective software solutions.[44] However, with regard to the single market approach the existence of different regimes within the EU was considered as counterproductive and therefore the harmonization of spam regulation was aimed for.

The labeling requirements of Article 7(1) of the E-Commerce Directive will apply next to the requirements of the E-Privacy Directive. For non-harmonized situations in which Member States will choose the opt-out regime, Article 7(2) on opt-out registers applies as well.

The E-Commerce Directive uses the notion 'commercial communications' as defined in Article 2(f) of the E-Commerce Directive. That notion does not have the same meaning as the notion 'direct marketing' which is used in the E-Privacy Directive. This is rather confusing since the two Directives are both applicable to different kinds of unsolicited electronic mail.

---

[43] Schaub 2002, p. 6.
[44] Report on the proposal for the E-Privacy Directive 2001, July 2001, pp. 18, 30-31.

1.7   CONCLUSIONS

In this chapter we have introduced our main research questions and the main objectives of this study. We have seen that it is hard to catch spam in a definition. We have established that spam must be seen from both an economic point of view and from a human rights point of view. We have noted the cross-over between spam and viruses. If spam is so hard to define, it will be also difficult to regulate it on a detailed level. Recital 40 of the E-Privacy Directive points to an approach to spam based on quality and the principle of permission, and not on quantity, which would use the notion of 'bulk' as a defining factor.

We have also described the complex relation between some fundamental rights and spam. We have introduced the spam triangle in order to describe the different roles and perspectives of the Internet Service Providers, the spammers and the end users. Different reasons to object to spam have a distinct legal translation. The regulation of spam is itself a multi-layered multi-focus project.

Since the E-Privacy Directive does not give a closed definition of spam it is up to the Member States, and eventually to the courts, to decide what exactly is spam in the spirit of the E-Privacy Directive and what is not. There have been a number of Directives that addressed the problem of unsolicited communications. The most explicit is the E-Commerce Directive. This is the first Directive to explicitly mention electronic mail, and to contain provisions on unsolicited commercial communications by electronic mail. The labeling requirements stated in Article 7(1) will operate in complement to the requirements of the E-Privacy Directive. In non-harmonized situations Article 7(2) might also apply. Since not all Member States have already implemented the Directives described in this chapter, the implementation of the E-Privacy Directive will provide them with a chance to catch up with the regulation of unsolicited communications. However, already before the E-Commerce Directive, the ISDN Privacy Directive introduced an opt-in regime for some forms of unsolicited communications.

Chapter 2
ARTICLE 13

Chapter 2
ARTICLE 13

2.1 THE NEW FRAMEWORK

In this chapter, we will assess the meaning of Article 13 of the E-Privacy Directive. We will be answering sub-questions 2 and 3 as presented in the first chapter, i.e., what is the scope of Article 13 in terms of object, subject and addressee and what are the weak spots or gray areas that this article creates.

First, we must describe the background to the E-Privacy Directive in order to present the context of the present regulatory regime. After the European IT summit in Lisbon, the Commission proposed a package of measures for a new regulatory framework for electronic communications.[45] This package followed partly from the 1999 Review of the electronic communications sector. The new regulatory framework altered the discourse from classical telecommunications to electronic communications. The e-communications framework is comprised of a general framework directive and four specific directives.[46] In its proposal for a common regulatory frame-

---

[45] The Lisbon Strategy was agreed upon by EU heads of state and government in March 2000 and has the objective of making the EU the most competitive and dynamic knowledge-based economy in the world by 2010. The strategy was a response to challenges faced by Europe in 2000, such as competition from the US and Asia and declining population growth. It aims to strengthen the EU's economy, driving job creation alongside social and environmental policies that ensure sustainable development and social inclusion. For more on the Lisbon Strategy, see <http://europa.eu.int/growthandjobs/index_en.htm>.

[46] Directive 2002/21/EC of the European Parliament and of the Council of 7 March 2002 on a common regulatory framework for electronic communications networks and services (Framework Directive), *OJ* L 108, 24.04.2002, p. 33. Besides the E-Privacy Directive, the other three specific directives are: Directive 2002/20/EC of the European Parliament and of the Council of 7 March 2002 on the authorization of electronic communications networks and services (Authorization Directive), Directive 2002/19/EC of the European

work for electronic communications networks and services, the European
Commission stated:

> 'The existing [now former] legislative framework was primarily de-
> signed to manage the transition from monopoly to competition and was
> therefore focused on the creation of a competitive market and the rights
> of new entrants. It has been successful in achieving those aims. But in
> part because of the success of liberalization at European level, the mar-
> ket is now changing with ever-increasing speed. This was foreseen by
> the current legislative framework, which required the Commission to
> review the operation of the Directives making up the regulatory frame-
> work in the light of developments in the market, the evolution in tech-
> nology and the changes in user demand. The new policy framework
> needs to take account of these developments, in particular the conver-
> gence between telecommunications, broadcasting and IT sectors. It
> seeks to reinforce competition in all market segments, while ensuring
> that the basic rights of consumers continue to be protected. It is there-
> fore designed to cater for new, dynamic and largely unpredictable mar-
> kets with many more players than today.'[47]

According to the Communication, the proposed Directive aims to establish
a harmonized regulatory framework for electronic communications networks
and services across the EU.

With regard to privacy and data protection in the communications sector, the Commission noted in its Communication following the 1999 Communications Review and Orientations for the new Regulatory Framework:

> 'the support in the consultation for updating the telecom data protection di-
> rective, will introduce proposals to ensure that data protection rules in the
> communications sector are technologically neutral and robust. In this context,
> it will examine in particular existing terms and definitions of the Directive

---

Parliament and of the Council of 7 March 2002 on access to, and interconnection of, electronic communications networks and associated facilities (Access Directive), Directive 2002/
22/EC of the European Parliament and of the Council of 7 March 2002 on universal service
and users' rights relating to electronic communications networks and services (Universal
Service Directive).

[47] Proposal for a common regulatory framework for electronic communications networks and services, COM(2000) 393 final 2000/0184 (COD), pp. 3-4.

and the consistency of coverage of old and new telecommunications services with new functionalities embedded in networks or software.'[48]

A proposal for a Directive concerning the processing of personal data and the protection of privacy in the electronic communications sector was subsequently issued, which lead to the adoption of the E-Privacy Directive in July 2002.

The e-communications framework was due for implementation on 25 July 2003. The E-Privacy Directive was adopted a few months later and did not have to be implemented until 31 October 2003. The Framework Directive is, *inter alia*, relevant for this study as it defines a number of important concepts that are used in the E-Privacy Directive. Article 2 of the E-Privacy Directive refers to the Framework Directive as a general set of definitions. A monitoring report of the E-Privacy Directive by the Commission is due before 2006.[49]

2.2   E-PRIVACY DIRECTIVE

Article 1 Scope and aim

1. This Directive harmonizes the provisions of the Member States required to ensure an equivalent level of protection of fundamental rights and freedoms, and in particular the right to privacy, with respect to the processing of personal data in the electronic communication sector and to ensure the free movement of such data and of electronic communication equipment and services in the Community.

---

[48] Communication of the European Commission, The results of the public consultation on the 1999 Communications Review and Orientations for the new Regulatory Framework, COM (2000) 239 final, p. 26. Available at <http://europa.eu.int/ISPO/infosoc/telecompolicy/en/com2000-239en.pdf>.

[49] In the Dutch Presidency Paper on unsolicited communications for direct marketing purposes, it was suggested that the review of the E-Privacy must not be postponed to the end of 2006, but needed to be started shortly in 2005. However, the Council Conclusions on unsolicited communications for direct marketing purposes adopted shortly after the submission of the Presidency Paper, does not change the date of review, nor are there any other signs in this direction. *Presidency Paper 2004*, p. 5.

> 2. The provisions of this Directive particularize and complement Directive 95/46/EC for the purposes mentioned in paragraph 1. Moreover, they provide for protection of the legitimate interests of subscribers who are legal persons.
> 3. This Directive shall not apply to activities which fall outside the scope of the Treaty establishing the European Community, such as those covered by Titles V and VI of the Treaty on European Union, and in any case to activities concerning public security, defence, State security (including the economic well-being of the State when the activities relate to State security matters) and the activities of the State in areas of criminal law.

The E-Privacy Directive replaced the Telecommunications Privacy Directive with regard to regulation of privacy within the telecommunication sector. The European Commission stated in its initial proposal:

> 'The Directive is one element in a new regulatory framework which seeks to ensure that the electronic communications sector continues to develop as a competitive market delivering benefits to all companies and individuals in the Community that use electronic communications services. The aim is to cover all electronic communications services in a technology neutral fashion. A harmonized level of data protection in the electronic communications sector is an essential element for the functioning of the internal market in electronic communications services and networks.'[50]

The basis for the E-Privacy Directive was provided by Article 95 of the Treaty establishing the European Community: measures relating to the establishment and functioning of the internal market. In order to improve the functioning of the internal market, the Member States of the European Union decided to harmonize privacy law on a European level and therefore to give up part of their autonomy. However, since privacy is a very sensitive topic among the Member States, the E-Privacy Directive, as the outcome of difficult negotiations among Member States, is a complex political compro-

---

[50] Proposal for a Directive of the European Parliament and of the Council concerning the processing of personal data and the protection of privacy in the electronic communications sector /* COM/2000/0385 final – COD 2000/0189 */ *OJ* C 365 E, 19.12.2000, p. 223 (under: Impact Assessment).

mise. Apart from that, a minimum level of harmonization was aimed for. Member States are indeed allowed to impose a stronger regime of protection, leaving Member States a lot of room to maintain their own national standards while implementing the Directive. In the process of that implementation, Member States interpret the Directive and transpose that interpretation into national legislation. To facilitate this interpretation the European Commission can put forward guidelines for implementation (as this kind of regulation is largely non-binding it is also called soft-law). The Communication on unsolicited communications or 'spam' of January 2004 is an example of the latter.[51] Ultimately, the European Court of Justice has the final say regarding the meaning of the Directive. So far, no cases pertaining to the interpretation of the E-Privacy Directive have been submitted to the European Court of Justice.[52]

The E-Privacy Directive contains provisions on a number of issues such as security of networks and services, confidentiality of communications, cookies, data retention, calling line identification, public subscriber directories and unsolicited communications. We must focus on Article 13 which regulates unsolicited communications but we will also discuss some other provisions related to the spam problem.

2.3   ARTICLE 13

The general rule on unsolicited e-mail has been laid down in Article 13 of the E-Privacy Directive. Article 13 is the result of a fierce battle of interests within and between the European Parliament and the Commission.

---

[51] Communication from the Commission to the European parliament, the Council, the European Economic and Social Committee and the Committee of the Regions on unsolicited commercial communications or 'spam', 22 January 2004, COM (2004) 28.

[52] A worried internet user and founder of the internetsite internet.libre.net, started a procedure for annulment of Art. 13(1), (2) and (3) of Directive 2002/58, but the action was dismissed as inadmissible. According to the court, Directive 2002/58 concerns the applicant only in his objective capacity as an internet user, in the same way as all other business users of the internet. The contested provisions of Directive 2002/58 cannot be regarded as of individual concern to the applicant because he fulfils none of the conditions of admissibility laid down by the fourth paragraph of Article 230 EC. *Vannieuwenhuyze-Morin* v. *Parliament and Council*, Order of the Court of First Instance of 6 May 2003, in Case T-321/02.

Article 13 'Unsolicited communications'

(1) The use of automated calling systems without human intervention (automatic calling machines), facsimile machines (fax) or electronic mail for the purposes of direct marketing may only be allowed in respect of subscribers who have given their prior consent.

(2) Notwithstanding paragraph 1, where a natural or legal person obtains from its customers their electronic contact details for electronic mail, in the context of the sale of a product or a service, in accordance with Directive 95/46/EC, the same natural or legal person may use these electronic contact details for direct marketing of its own similar products or services provided that customers clearly and distinctly are given the opportunity to object, free of charge and in an easy manner, to such use of electronic contact details when they are collected and on the occasion of each message in case the customer has not initially refused such use.

(3) Member States shall take appropriate measures to ensure that, free of charge, unsolicited communications for purposes of direct marketing, in cases other than those referred to in paragraphs 1 and 2, are not allowed either without the consent of the subscribers concerned or in respect of subscribers who do not wish to receive these communications, the choice between these options to be determined by national legislation.

(4) In any event, the practice of sending electronic mail for purposes of direct marketing disguising or concealing the identity of the sender on whose behalf de communication is made, or without a valid address to which the recipient may send a request that such communications cease, shall be prohibited.

(5) Paragraphs 1 and 3 shall apply to subscribers who are natural persons. Member States shall also ensure, in the framework of Community law and applicable national legislation, that the le-

> gitimate interests of subscribers other than natural persons with regard to unsolicited communications are sufficiently protected.

2.4   SCOPE I: UNSOLICITED COMMUNICATIONS

Unsolicited communication as a term reflects more than just e-mail. Unsolicited voice-mail messages, faxes, sms, unexpected pop-ups on computers and television commercials can also be perceived as spam. Article 13(1) mentions the following types of electronic communication: automatic calling machines, faxes and electronic mail. Article 13(2) and Article 13(4) refer to electronic mail. Article 13(3) and 13(5) refer to the notion of 'communications'. In order to be able to assess what rules apply to what type of communication we need to assess which types of unsolicited communications fall within the scope of Article 13 of the E-Privacy Directive.

Article 13(1) of the E-Privacy Directive lists automatic calling machines, fax machines and electronic mail as types of unsolicited communication to which the opt-in regime of the E-Privacy Directive applies. As a result of the Directives that preceded the E-Privacy Directive (see 2.1 above) automatic voice-mail messages and junk faxes no longer pose huge problems. This section will therefore focus on the question of which other types of unsolicited communication fall within the scope of the E-Privacy Directive. We will therefore look at the meaning of the notions of 'communication' and 'electronic mail' for the purposes of the E-Privacy Directive. We will start with the more general notion 'communication' of which electronic mail is a specific category.

Article 2(d) of the E-Privacy Directive defines 'communication' for the purpose of the E-Privacy Directive as follows:

Article 2(d)

'communication' means any information exchanged or conveyed between a finite numbers of parties by means of a publicly available electronic communications service. This does not include any information conveyed as part of a broadcasting service to the public over an electronic communications network except to the extent that the information can be related to the identifiable subscriber or user receiving the information.

Recital 16 of the E-Privacy Directive adds to this:

> **Recital 16**
>
> Information that is part of a broadcasting service provided over a public communications network is intended for a potentially unlimited audience and does not constitute a communication in the sense of this Directive. However, in cases where the individual subscriber or user receiving such information can be identified, for example with video-on-demand services, the information conveyed is covered within the meaning of a communication for the purposes of this Directive.

The exclusion of information which is part of a broadcasting service and aimed at a potentially unlimited audience, unless the recipient can be identified, makes the difference between the notion of 'communication' in the E-Privacy Directive and the meaning of the general notion of 'electronic communications', which can be derived from the definitions within the Framework Directive of 'electronic communications network'[53] and 'electronic communications service',[54] which both include broadcasting. The phrase 'a finite number of parties' in the definition of 'communication' in the E-Privacy Directive seems to aim at point-to-point communication. For

---

[53] Art. 2(a) Framework Directive provides that: 'electronic communications network' means transmission systems and, where applicable, switching or routing equipment and other resources which permit the conveyance of signals by wire, by radio, by optical or by other electromagnetic means, including satellite networks, fixed (circuit- and packet-switched, including Internet) and mobile terrestrial networks, electricity cable systems, to the extent that they are used for the purpose of transmitting signals, networks used for radio and television broadcasting, and cable television networks, irrespective of the type of information conveyed.

[54] Art. 2(c) Framework Directive provides that: 'electronic communications service' means a service normally provided for remuneration which consists wholly or mainly in the conveyance of signals on electronic communications networks, including telecommunications services and transmission services in networks used for broadcasting, but exclude services providing, or exercising editorial control over, content transmitted using electronic communications networks and services; it does not include information society services, as defined in Article 1 of Directive 98/34/EC, which do not consist wholly or mainly in the conveyance of signals on electronic communications networks.

this kind of communication an address is required, both to send and receive the communication.

A specific category of communication is electronic mail. According to Article 2(h) of the E-Privacy Directive 'electronic mail' means the following:

> **Article 2(h)**
>
> 'electronic mail' means any text, voice sound or image message sent over a public communications network which can be stored in the network or on the recipient's terminal equipment until it is collected by the recipient.

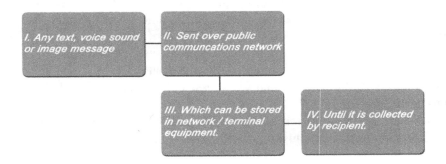

To find out what types of electronic communication are included within the notion 'electronic mail' we turn to the preparation of the E-Privacy Directive.

The original version of Article 2(h) contained the phrase 'which is addressed directly or indirectly to one or more natural or legal persons'[55] , instead of 'until it is collected by the recipient'. By contrast, an earlier version of Article 13 (1) stated:

---

[55] Report on the proposal for the E-Privacy Directive 2001, July 2001, p. 58.

> ## Article 13(1) earlier version
>
> The use of automated calling systems without human interven-
> tion (automatic calling machines), facsimile machines (fax) or
> electronic mail *and other personally addressed electronic com-
> munications* for the purposes of direct marketing may only be al-
> lowed in respect of subscribers who have given their prior con-
> sent.

The justification for the addition of the phrase 'other personally addressed
electronic communications' in this earlier version was the following: 'With
the huge expansion of mobile Internet products, services such as SMS are
already being abused by direct marketers. Europe has been the world leader
in mobile telephony. To allow direct marketers to abuse the service would
be to reduce its attractiveness to European consumers. For the interests of
the protection of personal data and the growth of electronic and mobile
commerce, there is an overwhelming case in favor of a ban on unsolicited
e-mail and other personally addressed messages in the EU.'[56] Nonetheless,
the addition 'and other personally addressed electronic communications'
has been removed.

Discussing the exclusion of electronic mail from the opt-in regime of
Article 13(1), and the inclusion of SMS, the Council stated:

> 'with protection of the subscriber and of technological neutrality in mind, the
> Council thought that the subscriber consent arrangements should embrace *ev-
> ery use of electronic mail* for the purposes of direct marketing purposes, and
> not just SMS.'

The Commission commented on this by stating:

> 'EP amendment 35 proposed to only single out SMS messages and include
> them in paragraph 1 of this article requiring prior consent of recipients while
> leaving the approach to *other forms of e-mail* for the Member States to de-
> cide. The Council preferred a harmonised approach on the basis of prior con-
> sent for *all forms of electronic mail*.'[57]

---

[56] Ibid., p. 71.
[57] Communication from the Commission to the European Parliament concerning the
common position of the Council on the adoption of the E-Privacy Directive, p. 71.

The preparation of the E-Privacy Directive showed two other interesting points. First, electronic mail seems to have been characterized as a personally addressed message. Second, the use of the notion 'electronic mail' has been rather inconsistent throughout the preparation of the Directive.

Another possible point of critique is that Article 13 on unsolicited communications, and the concepts related thereto, such as 'direct marketing' and 'communication', are connected to content. This is in itself inconsistent with the Framework which is supposed to regulate transmission, not the transmitted message, in a technology neutral fashion, as the Commission stated in its proposal for the Framework Directive:

'The proposed Directive is part of a package of five Directives and one Decision intended to reform the existing regulatory framework for electronic communications services and networks in the Community. One of the aims of this overall reform is to create rules which are technology neutral. The legal framework must try to ensure that services are regulated in an equivalent manner, irrespective of the technological means by which they are delivered. This also implies that consumers and users should get the same level of protection regardless of the technology used by particular service. Maintaining a high level of data protection and privacy for citizens is one of the declared aims of the current review'.[58]

Since Article 13 of the E-Privacy Directive specifically refers to electronic mail, there is no doubt that the Directive applies to e-mail. E-mail can contain different kinds of information, 'any text, voice sound or image message'. Also, e-mail is sent over the internet which is a public communications network.[59] 'Which can be stored in the network or on the recipient's termi-

---

[58] Ibid., pp. 1-2.

[59] Art. 2(d) of the Framework Directive defines 'public communications network' as follows: an electronic communications network used wholly or mainly for the provision of publicly available electronic communications services'. The definition of Art. 2(a) on 'electronic communications network' specifically mentions internet as a network: 'electronic communications network' means transmission systems and, where applicable, switching or routing equipment and other resources which permit the conveyance of signals by wire, by radio, by optical or by other electromagnetic means, including satellite networks, fixed (circuit- and packet-switched, including Internet) and mobile terrestrial networks, electricity cable systems, to the extent that they are used for the purpose of transmitting signals, networks used for radio and television broadcasting, and cable television networks, irrespective of the type of information conveyed.

nal equipment': anything can in principle be stored on terminal equipment, provided it has the appropriate functionality. Finally, '[U]ntil it is collected by the recipient': before an e-mail user pulls e-mail messages into the inbox of an e-mail program on his computer, the e-mail is stored on the mail-server. It is possible to leave e-mail on the server to be able to use it as an archive when working with web mail or to retrieve e-mail from the server at different locations, e.g., at home and at work.

Short Message Service ('SMS'), addressed to a mobile phone number, is a specific type of unsolicited communication falling within the scope of Article 13(1) and 13 as a whole. Recital 15 states that:

> **Recital 15**
>
> A communication may include any naming, numbering or ad-dressing information provided by the sender of a communication or the user of a connection to carry out the communication.

Recital 40 explicitly mentions SMS as a subcategory of e-mail.

> **Recital 40**
>
> Safeguards should be provided for subscribers against intrusion of their privacy by unsolicited communications for direct market-ing purposes in particular by means of automated calling ma-chines, telefaxes, and e-mails, including SMS messages (...).

SMS fits the criteria as well and falls within the definition of 'electronic mail'. SMS is delivered directly to the telephone of individual users, which are identified by their unique numbers. SMS qualifies as an instrument of direct-marketing. Therefore, unsolicited SMS messages of a commercial nature are covered by the opt-in regime of Article 13(1). The analysis in this subparagraph applies *mutatis mutandis* to similar technologies with different specifications, such as Multi Media Messaging (MMS).

2.5   SCOPE II: DIRECT MARKETING

There is no definition of direct marketing in either the specific or general Data Protection Directives. There is however a description of 'marketing purposes' in Recital 30 of Directive 95/46/EC on Data Protection:

> **Recital 30 DPD**
>
> (...) whereas Member States may similarly specify the conditions under which personal data may be disclosed to a third party for the purposes of marketing whether carried out commercially or by a charitable organization or by any other association or foundation, of a political nature for example, subject to the provisions allowing a data subject to object to the processing of data regarding him, at no cost and without having to state his reasons.

The Article 29 Working Party has stated that Article 13 of Directive 2002/58/EC consequently covers any form of sales promotion, including direct marketing by charities and political organizations (e.g., fund raising, etc.).[60]

During the preparatory process of the E-Privacy Directive, a Recital explaining to what extent the provisions on unsolicited communications for direct marketing purposes would affect messages sent by political parties and charities, was deleted. This Recital stated as follows:

> **Recital 44 (deleted)**
>
> Direct marketing activities carried out by political, charity or other organizations, for instance activities aimed at recruiting new members, fund-raising or lobbying for votes, are included in the concept of direct marketing as established by Directive 95/46/EC. Messages by political organizations or others for purposes other than direct marketing, for example the expression of views, thoughts and ideas, are not covered by the provisions on unsolicited communications of this Directive.

---

[60] Art. 29 Working Party 2004, p. 7.

This Recital was deleted by the European Parliament, because of the fact that

> 'the distinction introduced between direct marketing activities ("aimed at re-
> cruiting new members, fund raising or lobbying for votes") and other activi-
> ties ("expression of views, thoughts and ideas") is artificial since these activi-
> ties – that are at the basis of and a reason for the existence of associations,
> charities and parties – are intermingled and linked between each other.'[61]

According to the Commission, the Recital only clarified an existing interpretation under the Data Protection Directive and its deletion does not
mean a change of substance, only a 'lesser degree of transparency that is
acceptable than is acceptable as part of the overall compromise package.'[62] (Political) ideas are more strongly protected under the flag of freedom of expression than speech of a more obvious commercial nature.
Political parties, charities or other organizations, which send out messages
solely expressing views, thoughts and ideas without a direct commercial
aim therefore fall outside the scope of Article 13 of the E-Privacy Directive. Nevertheless, according to Recital 10 and Article 1(2) of the E-Privacy Directive, these communications are still covered by the general regime
on data-processing of the Data Protection Directive.

If we compare this to the current definitions of advertising, we find that,
according to Article 2 of the Directive on Misleading Advertising, the notion 'advertising' means the following:

Article 2 Directive on Misleading Advertising

'Advertising' means: the making of a representation in any form
in connection with a trade, business, craft or profession in order
to promote the supply of goods or services, including immovable
property, rights and obligations.[63]

---

[61] EP Recommendation for a second reading on the common position on the E-Privacy
Directive, April 2002, p. 11.

[62] Opinion of the Commission amending the proposal for the E-Privacy Directive, June
2002, p. 4.

[63] Council Directive 84/450/EEC of 10 September 1984 relating to the approximation
of the laws, regulations and administrative provisions of the Member States concerning
misleading advertising, *OJ* L 250, 19.09.1984, p. 17.

The key element of advertising is the promotion of the supply of goods and services.

Article 2(f) of the E-Commerce Directive defines commercial communication as follows:

> **Article 2(f) E-Commerce Directive**
>
> 'commercial communication' means any form of communication designed to promote, directly or indirectly, the goods, services or image of a company, organization or person pursuing a commercial, industrial, or craft activity or exercising a regulated profession.

The phrase 'directly or indirectly' can be interpreted either to include direct marketing in the category of commercial communications or to include communications with an indirect commercial aim such as communications by political parties or charities.

The 1985 Recommendation of the Council of Europe on the protection of personal data used for the purposes of direct marketing defines 'direct marketing' as: 'all activities which make it possible to offer goods or services or to transmit any other messages to a segment of the population by post, telephone or other direct means aimed at informing or soliciting a response from the data subject as well as any service ancillary thereto.'[64] In this definition of direct marketing the phrases 'segment of the population' and 'direct means' are the distinctive elements.

The European Code of Practice for the Use of Personal Data in Direct Marketing of the Federation of European Direct Marketing (FEDMA),[65] which has been approved by the Article 29 Working Party,[66] defines direct marketing as: 'the communication by whatever means (including but not limited to mail, fax, telephone, on-line services etc. ...) of any advertising or marketing material, which is carried out by the Direct Marketer itself or on its behalf and which is directed to particular individuals.'

---

[64] 1985 Recommendation of the Council of Europe on the protection of personal data used for the purposes of direct marketing, p. 2.

[65] FEDMA's Code of Practice, p. 3.

[66] Art. 29 Working Party 2003.

This definition is technology neutral and applies to e-mail, SMS or other means of communication. The phrase 'which is carried out by the Direct Marketer itself or on its behalf', within the definition of direct marketing of the FEDMA Code, does justice to the fact that most spam runs are handled by agents instead of by vendors themselves. The FEDMA Code further defines the notion 'direct marketer' as: 'any natural or legal person (including charities and political parties) who communicates by whatever means (including but not limited to mail, fax, telephone, on-line services etc. ...) any advertising or marketing material which is directed to particular individuals.' The key phrase in the definition of direct marketing in the FEDMA Code is therefore 'directed to particular individuals'.

Once we look at the distinguishing elements of the various definitions addressed here, it is relevant to assess what distinguishes direct marketing from commercial communications in general. 'Marketing' seems to refer to the promotion of goods or services. The promotion of image seems not to be included since we have seen earlier in this section that messages reflecting ideas, without a direct commercial aim, seem to be exempted from Article 13 of the E-Privacy Directive.

Crucial in distinguishing direct marketing from commercial communications in general is the manner in which the promotion reaches its target. In direct marketing the promotional message is delivered to a limited group of potential customers, as opposed to a potentially unlimited audience that can be reached through a mass medium, e.g., broadcasting or a newspaper. To reach a limited group of potential customers, the message has to be addressed in order to be delivered on an individual basis. For the message to be addressed it is not necessary that the addressees name is stated, or that the message is individualized. The prerequisite of an address distinguishes direct marketing from advertising in general. In short, within the E-Privacy Directive, the notion 'direct marketing' seems to point to the promotion of goods and services by means of addressed messages.

2.6 OPT-IN

Like its predecessor, the ISDN Directive, Article 13 of the E-Privacy Directive requires prior consent for the use of *automatic calling machines and faxes* for the purposes of direct marketing. Now, also electronic mail has been placed under an opt-in regime. Opt-in requires prior consent, meaning that the recipient has to give his permission to send him communications, beforehand. This is the mirror image of the opt-out option, when the recipient can only refuse permission to send him any further communications after receipt of an unsolicited communication.

The disadvantages of an opt-out regime are many (or: great). First, it can take a lot of effort to opt-out on every unsolicited communication a person may receive. Secondly, opting-out offers the spammer evidence that the used contact details are correct, making them even more valuable. Even if the organization which keeps the opt-out register is legitimate and does not use or sell the registered contact details, there is still the danger that the register will be hacked. A database with confirmed contact details is even more valuable to spammers than e-mail addresses which are harvested on the internet and which sometimes are out of date.

Opt-in can be made stronger by applying a so-called double opt-in standard. Double opt-in requires the following procedure: after a user has given his consent, a message is sent to this user (by e-mail or SMS). The user then has to reply to this message, for instance by following a link to a web site and entering a code which has been included in the message. The user then receives a message which contains the final confirmation of the opt-in. This way it is harder to sign up with someone else's address.

The term 'soft opt-in' has been used to describe the main exception to Article 13(1), namely Article 13(2). It has been called soft opt-in because it presupposes a prior relationship between the sender and the recipient of the message. In that case a 'softer' regime applies than the one in Article 13(1). The recipient has already provided the sender with his contact details in the context of a previous relationship and has at that time agreed to receive unsolicited messages, so no further action is required.

2.6.1   13(1): Prior consent

What are the requirements for prior consent? Article 2(f) of the E-Privacy Directive states that consent by a user or subscriber corresponds to the data subject's consent in the Data Protection Directive.[67] According to Article 2(h) of the Data Protection Directive 'the data subject's consent' shall mean

---

[67] See also Recital 17 of the E-Privacy Directive.

any freely given specific and informed indication of his wishes by which the data subject signifies his agreement to personal data relating to him being processed.

There may be various ways by which consent may be provided in accordance with Community law. The actual method to collect that consent has not been specifically provided for in Directive 2002/58/EC. Recital 17 re-affirms this:

> **Recital 17**
>
> (...) Consent may be given by any appropriate method enabling a freely given specific and informed indication of the user's wishes, including by ticking a box when visiting an Internet web site.

Without prejudice to other applicable requirements on, e.g., information, methods whereby a subscriber gives prior consent by registering on a web site and is later asked to confirm that he was the person who registered and to confirm his consent seem to be compatible with the Directive. Other methods may also be compatible with legal requirements.

In our opinion however, this does not include 'unticking a box'. Furthermore, since the consent has to be given by the data subject itself, 'tell a friend' is not a valid method to inform potential customers. Interpretation of the notion 'consent' is a matter of civil law, and therefore the meaning of consent can differ among Member States.

According to the Article 29 Working Party, it would not be compatible with Article 13 of Directive 2002/58/EC simply to ask, by a general e-mail sent to recipients, their consent to receive marketing e-mails, because of the requirement that the purpose for which the consent is sought be legitimate, explicit and specific.[68]

> 'Moreover, consent given on the occasion of the general acceptance of the terms and conditions governing the possible main contract (e.g., a subscription contract, in which consent is also sought to send communications for direct marketing purposes) must respect the requirements in Directive 95/46/

---

[68] Art. 29 Working Party 2004, p. 5.

EC, that is, be informed, specific and freely given. Provided that these latter conditions are met, consent might be given by the data subject for instance, through the ticking of a box.'[69]

Ultimately, this is a matter of national law to be solved by national legislators.

The purposes of the required consent should also be unmistakably indicated.

'This implies that the goods and services, or the categories of goods and services, for which marketing e-mails may be sent should be clearly indicated to the subscriber. Consent to pass on the personal data to third parties should also be asked where applicable. The information provided to the data subject should therefore indicate the purpose(s), and the goods and services (or categories of goods and services) for which those third parties would end e-mails.'[70]

As stated by the Article 29 Working Party, lists of e-mail addresses which have not been established according to the prior consent requirement may not be used anymore under the opt-in regime, at least until they have been adapted to the new requirements.[71]

'Selling such incompatible lists to third parties is not legal either. Companies wishing to buy lists of e-mail addresses should be cautious that those lists are in accordance with applicable requirements, and in particular that prior consent was given in accordance with those requirements. However, it is a matter for national law to decide the exact rules on e-mail lists within the Directive's framework.'[72]

Article 13 also provides for the obligation to offer an opt-out possibility in each message sent. Such an opt-out should at least be possible using the same communications service (e.g., by sending an SMS to opt-out of an SMS-based marketing list).[73]

---

[69] Idem.
[70] Idem.
[71] Art. 29 Working Party 2004, p. 6.
[72] Idem.
[73] Art. 29 Working Party 2004, p. 7.

2.6.2   13(2): Soft opt-in

As mentioned above, Article 13(2) presents an exception to the opt-in regime of Article 13(1), with regard to existing customer relations. When a
company has acquired the electronic contact details of a customer in the
context of a sale, the company can send this person unsolicited messages
for purposes of direct marketing of its own products or services, unless this
person objected to this at the time the contact details were acquired. The
recipient of the unsolicited message can then opt-out if he no longer wants
to receive such messages. Recital 41 explains Article 13(2) as follows:

> **Recital 41**
>
> Within the context of an existing customer relationship, it is rea-
> sonable to allow the use of electronic contact details for the of-
> fering of similar products or services, but only by the same com-
> pany that has obtained the electronic contact details in accor-
> dance with Directive 95/46/EC. When electronic contact details
> are obtained, the customer should be informed about their further
> use for direct marketing in a clear and distinct manner, and be
> given the opportunity to refuse such usage. This opportunity
> should continue to be offered with each subsequent direct mar-
> keting message, free of charge, except for any costs for the trans-
> mission of this refusal.

As both Article 13 and Recital 41 state, electronic contact details must be
processed in accordance with the principles of Directive 95/46 EC, the Data
Protection Directive. Electronic contact details are personal data since the
name of the customer will be registered as well. This renders it possible to
identify the person behind even the most non-descriptive e-mail address.
This means that, in order for the processing to be fair, the user of the electronic contact details must be provided with certain information before he
discloses his or her data, and must consent to the use to which it is to be put.
The information to be provided to him must include the identity of the data
controller, the purpose for which the data is to be processed and any further
information which is necessary, having regard to the specific circumstances

in which the data is or are to be processed, to enable processing in respect of the data subject to be fair.[74]

In practice, this means that when the electronic contact details are collected, information has to be provided about the natural or legal person that collects the data (the data controller). This includes information on whether the data is collected for the company itself, or for, e.g., a holding to which the company belongs. Also, it must be clear to the data subject that his contact details may be used for direct marketing purposes, so that customers have the opportunity to object to such use of their electronic contact details.

The fact that regard should be given to the specific circumstances in which the data is or are to be processed, may imply that there is an obligation to also provide information on the natural person or legal person who processes the data on behalf of the data controller (the data processor). This could pose difficulties to a company that wishes to hire another company to perform a direct marketing campaign on its behalf, after the data have been obtained. In some instances a company is required to have a privacy protocol, according to national law.

The text of Article 13(2) is unclear as regards the addresses obtained from customers before the entering into force of the E-Privacy Directive. Because the text of provision 13(2) is phrased in the present ('where a natural or legal person obtains from its customers their electronic contact details for electronic mail'), it seems unlikely that electronic contact details of previous customers can be used to send unsolicited commercial communications. Also, Article 13(2) demands that 'customers clearly and distinctly are given the opportunity to object, free of charge and in an easy manner, to such use of electronic contact details when they are collected'. As Recital 41 explains, use of electronic contact details is only allowed when the data controller, to comply with the prerequisites for fair processing of the Data Protection Directive as described in the previous section, has already informed his customers at the time their electronic contact details were collected, of the possible use of those data for the purposes of direct marketing. A company is not allowed to send unsolicited communications to customers who did not consent to this beforehand.[75] In the process of transposing

---

[74] Owen & Kiernan Earl 2003, p. 3.

[75] However, electronic addresses could be used to send unsolicited messages of an obvious non-commercial nature, such as safety warnings, which fall outside the scope of Art. 13.

the Directive, national laws should clarify this ambiguity. To provide for a transitional system in which previous customers can be asked for permission to send further unsolicited communications may be a violation of the rules laid down in Article 13 of the Directive, because the communication which is used to ask for permission to send further communications, would be an unsolicited communication in itself.

Article 13(2) relates to contact details obtained in the *context of a sale* of a product or a service. What is considered a sale? In an earlier draft the text stated 'purchase' instead of 'sale'. The text was amended because it was feared that marketers could argue that although no sale had taken place, a consumer could be approached under the soft opt-in regime, as they had expressed an interest in purchasing a product.[76] This indicates that there has to be a finalized sales contract, not just an order or a down-payment on a future sale.

If the sales contract is broken and the contract is subsequently nullified, it is a matter for national law to decide whether that means that there was never a relationship between consumer and supplier and that therefore the soft opt-in rule does not apply.

It is unclear for what period of time addresses of previous customers may be used for direct marketing purposes. Article 6(e) of the Data Protection Directive states that Member States shall provide that personal data must be 'kept in a form which permits identification of data subjects for no longer than is necessary for the purposes for which the data were collected or for which they are further processed.'

The term 'the context of the sale' suggests that contact details obtained from potential customers would fall in the soft opt-in exception. However, since the term 'purchase' was replaced by the term 'sale', details given *before* the sale can only be used if a sale eventually did take place. Therefore, addresses of potential buyers can only be used according to the opt-in rules of Article 13(1). Addresses of potential customers can be gathered through cookies that register people who are 'just browsing' on the web, and can register even the articles they are interested in.[77] Even if permission is obtained for the use of that kind of technology as is required under Article 5(3) of the E-Privacy Directive, this does not imply consent to send

---

[76] Magee 2003, p. 22.
[77] Idem.

unsolicited communications. Another way of collecting contact details from potential customers is when interested consumers request information about a certain product or service. Unless of course these future customers already gave their consent for further related marketing on the request form, it seems logical that the opt-in rule of Article 13(1) would apply here as well.[78]

Article 13(2) states that contact details may be used for direct marketing of a company's (or: the relevant natural or legal person's) own *similar products or services*. This immediately creates a number of questions of interpretation. It has to be established what this means for companies that sell thousands of different articles, whether a (web) store with different articles has the right to market every other item they sell, and whether the interpretation of 'similar' should be wide or narrow.

Another problem is the question whether different parts of a holding can be considered as one company and, for example, if retailers are allowed to use the soft-opt in regime. After all, Article 13(2) provides that contact details may be used for direct marketing of a company's *own* similar products and services.

Article 13(2) states in the first sentence 'where a natural or legal person *obtains* from *its* customers'. A previous version of the Directive stated that the electronic contact details had to be obtained directly from the customer in question. The removal of that explicit condition could indicate that a manufacturer or wholesaler, who has obtained an e-mail address from the retailer who made the sale, may regard the e-mail address as being that of one of its own customers.[79] However, Recital 41 states clearly that the use of electronic contact details is allowed 'only by the same company that has obtained the electronic contact details'. Depending on whether the name of the holding or the company is used on the consent form, this could mean that the concept of 'company' might not stretch beyond that particular company, or the holding the company belongs to. In case of transfer to third parties, the data subject should be notified according to Article 11 of the

---

[78] For a broader interpretation of the notion 'context of a sale', see Butler 2003 on the English implementation of the E-Privacy Directive. Note that the English implementation in this respect was broader than in our opinion was allowed. See also chapter 5.2.2.

[79] Magee 2003, p. 22.

Data Protection Directive. Again, however, this would be an unsolicited communication in itself.

Article 13(2) could become an area that could provoke a lot of case law. Whether products are similar, come from the same store or if the customer gave his address to this particular store are all questions to which the answers are different from case to case.

The addressee has to be able to opt out of future marketing, in an easy way and free of charge. However, it should be noted that the user of the address still has to pay to send that e-mail and spend time and effort on opting out. Recital 41 acknowledges this, but does not give the option of reimbursement.

It seems reasonable that the requirements for soft opt-in, namely 'the opportunity to object, free of charge and in an easy manner' also apply to customers who have opted in before and now want to opt-out. This should be provided for in a clear and distinct manner on the occasion of each message that is sent.

The soft opt-in provision exchanges the prerequisite of prior consent of Article 13(1) for a more general consent to the use of electronic contact details, which includes the use of such data for the purpose of direct marketing. The range of products a customer agrees to receive promotional messages on, may not be clear at the time the customer gives his consent, since Article 13(2) can be interpreted in a very broad sense, including all kinds of products from all kinds of companies that are related to the original collector of the data, which had a direct relationship with this customer. However, in its later Communication, the Commission has made it very clear that Article 13(2) is to be interpreted and implemented restrictively, in order to avoid effectively undermining the opt-in regime.[80] The Article 29 Working Party also stresses that the exception of Article 13(2) must be interpreted narrowly.[81]

2.7   13(3): OTHER UNSOLICITED COMMUNICATIONS

Member States must take appropriate measures regarding other unsolicited communications. The choice between the options set out in Article 13(3)

---

[80] Communication 2004, p. 9.
[81] Art. 29 Working Party 2004, p. 9.

seems to refer to the choice between an opt-in and an opt-out regime. Non-automatic calls by direct marketers are an example of 'other unsolicited communications'.

2.8   13(4): IDENTIFICATION

This article aims to ban the practice of falsifying the point of origin and transmission path of electronic mail to conceal the sender's identity. The requirement of a valid return address poses some questions. What is to be understood by 'valid'? Spam spread through hacked machines and their e-mail programs (and possibly their address book) and which therefore can contain an existing address may very well be using a valid address. Perhaps the validity of an address should be connected with its opt-out effectiveness.

The E-Commerce Directive also contains a requirement for the natural or legal person on whose behalf the commercial communication is made, to be clearly identifiable (Art. 6 (b)). Concerning the recognizability of the direct marketing message, the labeling requirements of Article 7(1) of the E-Commerce Directive will apply next to the requirements of the E-Privacy Directive. Commercial communication needs to be identifiable clearly and unambiguously as such as soon as it is received by the recipient.

2.9   13(5): USERS, SUBSCRIBERS, CORPORATIONS

Article 13(5) provides that paragraphs (1) and (3) shall apply to subscribers who are natural persons. While this Article requires Member States to take measures in order to protect the interests subscribers other than natural persons, they remain free to determine the appropriate safeguards to do so. It is left up to Member States to decide whether, for example, legal persons are protected by the opt-in rule of Article 13(1). This leaves Member States a wide margin of appreciation.

The fact that, in principle, Article 13(1) and (2) only protect *subscribers*, poses some questions. Consider, for instance, the head of a family who has a contract with an internet service provider to access the internet and to have an e-mail account. Such an account often has several addresses which

are distributed to members of that family. The mother and children are users but not subscribers. This means that only the father would be directly
protected by the opt-in regime and the measures taken on the bases of Article 13(3). In order to opt-in, the subscriber has to give his consent. Theo-
retically this would mean that the mother and children would have to ask
the father to opt-in for them.

Member States have to ensure that the legitimate interests of subscribers
other than natural persons are sufficiently protected. This points towards
protection of corporations. Users, like the other family members in our example who are natural persons but not subscribers, are therefore only protected under Article 13(2). However, some EU members have decided to
apply the opt-in regime also to persons that are not subscribers. For example, France does not protect subscribers as such, but the use of personal
data of a physical person to send commercial communications without consent. It does not matter if you are a subscriber, a company or a private
user.[82]

The Article 7(2) of the E-Commerce Directive applies in concurrence
with the E-Privacy Directive. The obligation to respect and consult opt-out
registers might therefore also be relevant to customers opting-out of unsolicited electronic communications based on existing customer relationships.
This includes users.

Legal persons are not protected by the general regime of the Data Protection Directive. The E-Privacy Directive does not oblige Member States
to extent the application of Directive 95/46/EC to the protection of the legitimate interests of legal persons.[83] However, Recital 45 of the E-Privacy
Directive states:

Recital 45

This Directive is without prejudice to the arrangements which
Member States make to protect the legitimate interests of legal
persons with regard to unsolicited communications for direct
marketing purposes. Where Member States establish an opt-out

---

[82] For more on the protection of corporate interests and the position of legal persons
under national law, see chapter 5.3.

[83] See Recital 12 of the E-Privacy Directive.

> register for such communications to legal persons, mostly busi-
> ness users, the provisions of Article 7 of Directive 2000/31/EC of
> the European Parliament and of the Council of 8 June 2000 on
> certain legal aspects of information society services, in particular
> electronic commerce, in the internal market (Directive on elec-
> tronic commerce) are fully applicable.

This means that Member States are obliged to protect corporations from
unsolicited communications, either by means of an opt-in or an opt-out
system. If Member States choose the opt-out system, the provisions of the
E-Commerce Directive apply.

The need for protection of corporations was already expressed in the
initial proposal for the E-Privacy Directive:

> 'Articles 12 and 13 on directories and unsolicited communications require
> Member States to take account of the legitimate interests of subscribers to
> electronic communications services who are legal persons, with regard to the
> publication of their data in public directories and with regard to possibilities
> to protect themselves against unsolicited communications for direct market-
> ing purposes. Those provisions recognize that small and medium sized firms
> may have similar problems as individuals in these two areas.'[84]

The fact that Article 13(5) states that the protection of Article 13(1) and
Article 13(3) applies to subscribers who are natural persons, seems to exclude all corporations. However, when a corporation consists of only one
person, in that case the subscriber might in fact be a natural person.
Freelancers for example, are often not legal persons. Most freelancers use
the same address for work and personal mail. Furthermore, employees can
also use their work address for non-work related communications, at home
as well as at work. In principle, they are left outside the scope of Article
13(5). The employer is the subscriber and as the employer in most cases
will be a legal person, Articles 13(1) and 13(3) do not apply. However,
paragraph 5 only relates to paragraphs 1 and 3 of Article 13 and Member
States are free to adopt an opt-in approach also for corporate subscribers or
other users. Also, Article 13(2) on existing customer relations refers to cus-

---

[84] Proposal for the E-Privacy Directive 2000, p. 30.

tomers who may opt-out of their e-mailings. The notion 'customers' comprises both individuals as well as organizations. Companies and their employees can therefore opt-out of business to business e-marketing.

The interests of subscribers other than natural persons have to be sufficiently protected by national law. Member States are free to arrange for a stronger protection for corporations. This has caused a lot of discussion in various Member States. Corporations obviously suffer from spam too. The argument that business to business marketing should stay possible could be met by giving employees the protection as offered by the opt-in requirements of Article 13(1). This would meet the needs of companies, while leaving strict business addresses like <info@corporation.com> susceptible to unsolicited communications. It is very important how the burden of proof is divided in situations like this. If, for instance, the spammer had the burden to prove that the spam receiver is in fact not a natural person and the subscriber, it would mean that spammers could not risk to keep sending spam to most corporate e-mail addresses. That would *de facto* broaden the opt-in rule to corporate e-mail accounts. The division of the burden of proof is a matter of national law.

2.10   CONCLUSIONS

In this chapter, we have discussed the specific regulation of unsolicited communications in the E-Privacy Directive. We have seen how the Directive fits within the framework on electronic communications that has been introduced in the EC. An important goal of the framework is to adapt former telecommunications law to the internet era and to provide for effective consumer protection. In that perspective, the Commission has more than once stressed the importance it attaches to protection against spam.

The E-Privacy Directive itself is the successor to the 1997 ISDN Privacy Directive and contains provisions on a number of issues related to privacy and communications. Article 13 provides for a harmonized protection against unsolicited communications or spam. The article has been the subject of a lot of debate between the European Parliament and the European Commission and the final text presents in some ways the results of that fierce struggle. The scope of Article 13 is defined by a number of key definitions. Article 13 only relates to unsolicited communications with direct marketing purposes. It is therefore important to find out the meaning and correct interpretation of 'direct marketing'.

Article 13(1) has introduced a pan European opt-in rule for unsolicited communications. It is a very important step in order to harmonize anti-spam laws throughout the Union. The opt-in rule means that spammers are only allowed to send their messages if they have received the prior consent of their addressees. The meaning of the concept of 'consent' is influenced by the meaning attached to consent in the Data Protection Directive. Article 13(2) introduces an exception to the main opt-in rule for sending information in the context of existing customer relations (or: to existing customers) concerning similar products or services. It is because of that exception that Article 13 was named 'soft opt-in' by some.

Article 13(3) provides for an obligation for Member States to ensure an adequate protection against other forms of unsolicited communications. Article 13(4) prohibits the use of false or disguised identity when sending direct marketing e-mails, while Article 13(5) requires Member States to take measures in order to protect the interests of subscribers other than natural persons. It is very important how the burden of proof is divided in situations where the opt-in rule does not apply to legal persons. If, for instance, the spammer has the burden to prove that the spam receiver is in fact not a natural person and the subscriber, it would mean that spammers could not risk to keep sending spam to most corporate e-mail addresses.

The scope of Article 13 is limited to natural persons being subscribers to the relevant electronic communications services. It is left up to Member States to decide whether legal persons and users which are not subscribers can also enjoy the protection of the opt-in rule of Article 13(1). This limited scope renders the article much less effective in providing adequate protection against spam as a lot of people receive most unsolicited communications while at work or at their work address.

Chapter 3
SPAM AND SECURITY

Chapter 3
SPAM AND SECURITY

3.1 INTRODUCTION

Spam can slow down computer networks and can seriously damage personal computers when used to spread computer viruses or worms. Large volumes of spam can even interfere with critical computer infrastructures and endanger public safety. Some spam also contains destructive viruses and worms. Virus writers sometimes write programs that download users' address books and propagate viruses by sending them to all users in an address book. That way, virus writers avoid anti-spam filters. Spammers also exploit security weaknesses inherent in e-mail transfer technology such as open relays and open proxies. Other security issues are raised by the use of spam to lure unsuspecting users to web pages where spying software is secretly downloaded. Spy ware monitors a user's activity on the Internet and transmits that information to someone else. It may also gather information about e-mail addresses, passwords, and credit-card numbers.[85]

In recent years, internet users have been plagued by combinations of spam and viruses. Spammers seem to be using virus-writing techniques to get their messages through filters. Virus writers also have made use of spammers' mass-mailing techniques for the purpose of attacking computer systems. Therefore, we need to assess the possible convergence in the regulation of viruses and spam via the rules on security.

Article 4 of the E-Privacy Directive provides, under circumstances, for a service and/or network provider to take appropriate technical and organizational measures to safeguard security of its services and/or networks. It is safe to assume that sometimes spam spread by a virus (and vice versa) is spam in the context of Article 13 of the E-Privacy Directive. If spam threatens the security of a network, it seems reasonable to infer that Article 4

---

[85] OECD 2004, pp. 16-17.

L.F. Asscher and S.A. Hoogcarspel, Regulating Spam
© 2006, T·M·C·ASSER PRESS, *The Hague, and the authors*

applies. In this chapter, we will analyze this specific section of the E-Privacy Directive dealing with network security and the possible obligations and liabilities of service and/ or network providers.

3.2   ARTICLE 4 AND THE PROCESSING OF PERSONAL DATA

Article 4 of the E-Privacy Directive provides as follows:

> **Article 4 'Security'**
>
> (1) The provider of a publicly available electronic communications service must take appropriate technical and organizational measures to safeguard security of its services, if necessary in conjunction with the provider of the public communications network with respect to network security. Having regard to the state of the art and the cost of their implementation, these measures shall ensure a level of security appropriate to the risk presented.
>
> (2) In case of a particular risk of a breach of the security of the network, the provider of a publicly available electronic communications service must inform the subscribers concerning such risk and, where the risk lies outside the scope of the measures to be taken by the service provider, of any possible remedies, including an indication of the likely costs involved.

The ratio and goals pursued by this article, are explained more in detail in Recital 20 of the E-Privacy Directive.

> **Recital 20**
>
> Service providers should take appropriate measures to safeguard the security of their services, if necessary in conjunction with the provider of the network, and inform subscribers of any special risks of a breach of the security of the network. Such risks may especially occur for electronic communications services over an open network such as the Internet or analogue mobile telephony.

It is particularly important for subscribers and users of such services to be fully informed by their service provider of the existing security risks which lie outside the scope of possible remedies by the service provider. Service providers who offer publicly available electronic communications services over the Internet should inform users and subscribers of measures they can take to protect the security of their communications for instance by using specific types of software or encryption technologies. The requirement to inform subscribers of particular security risks does not discharge a service provider from the obligation to take, at its own costs, appropriate and immediate measures to remedy any new, unforeseen security risks and restore the normal security level of the service. The provision of information about security risks to the subscriber should be free of charge except for any nominal costs which the subscriber may incur while receiving or collecting the information, for instance by downloading an electronic mail message. Security is appraised in the light of Article 17 of Directive 95/46/EC.

The Recital specifically states that security is appraised in the light of Article 17 of the Data Protection Directive. This prompts the question of what that means with regard to the notion of security as used in Article 4 of the E-Privacy Directive.

Article 17 Data Protection Directive pertains to the security of data when processed, in particular where the processing involves the transmission of data over a network.

Article 17 DPD 'Security of processing'

(1) Member States shall provide that the controller must implement appropriate technical and organizational measures to protect personal data against accidental or unlawful destruction or accidental loss, alteration, unauthorized disclosure or access, in particular where the processing involves the transmission of data over a network, and against all other unlawful forms of processing. Having regard to the state of the art and the cost of their implementation, such measures shall ensure a level of security

appropriate to the risks represented by the processing and the nature of the data to be protected.

(2) The Member States shall provide that the controller must, where processing is carried out on his behalf, choose a processor providing sufficient guarantees in respect of the technical security measures and organizational measures governing the processing to be carried out, and must ensure compliance with those measures.

(3) The carrying out of processing by way of a processor must be governed by a contract or legal act binding the processor to the controller and stipulating in particular that:
• the processor shall act only on instructions from the controller,
• the obligations set out in paragraph 1, as defined by the law of the Member State in which the processor is established, shall also be incumbent on the processor.

(4) For the purposes of keeping proof, the parts of the contract or the legal act relating to data protection and the requirements relating to the measures referred to in paragraph 1 shall be in writing or in another equivalent form

The controller must implement appropriate technical and organizational measures to protect personal data against unauthorized or unlawful processing, against accidental or unlawful destruction or accidental loss, alteration, unauthorized disclosure or access and all other unlawful forms of processing. The responsibility, and therefore the liability, lies with the controller. Article 2(d) of the Data Protection Directive defines 'controller' as follows:

Article 2(d) DPD

'controller' shall mean the natural or legal person, public authority, agency or any other body which alone or jointly with others determines the purposes and means of the processing of personal data; where the purposes and means of processing are determined

> by national or Community laws or regulations, the controller or the specific criteria for his nomination may be designated by national or Community law.

Data processing means, according to Article 2(c) of the Data Protection Directive:

> **Article 2(b) DPD**
>
> 'processing of personal data' ('processing') shall mean any operation or set of operations which is performed upon personal data, whether or not by automatic means, such as collection, recording, organization, storage, adaptation or alteration, retrieval, consultation, use, disclosure by transmission, dissemination or otherwise making available, alignment or combination, blocking, erasure or destruction.

Service providers process data in multiple ways: collection, use, storage etc. Therefore, they are processors within the meaning of the Data Protection Directive.

> **Article 2(e) DPD**
>
> 'processor' shall mean a natural or legal person, public authority, agency or any other body which processes personal data on behalf of the controller.

Besides processors, in the specific context of the E-Privacy Directive, providers are also controllers that are responsible for the security of the network or services and therefore of the data transport, including the data processing involved. Hence, they may be liable on the basis of Article 17 Data Protection Directive. Furthermore, if under specific circumstances, a provider cannot be considered the 'controller', but merely the 'processor', Article 17(3) of the Data Protection Directive creates a contractual obligation for the provider with regard to the controller, to process the data according to the standards of Article 17 of the Data Protection Directive.

3.3   'APPROPRIATE TECHNICAL AND ORGANIZATIONAL MEASURES'

As provided for in Article 4(1), the provider a publicly available electronic communications service must take appropriate technical and organizational measures to safeguard security of its services, if necessary in conjunction with the provider of the public communications network with respect to network security.

'Technical measures' refers to protective devices such as firewalls, but also to blocking and filtering of e-mail containing viruses. Since viruses can also operate as spam distributors, this obligation is relevant to the fight against spam. Article 4(1) also calls for organizational measures, for instance extra personnel for system analysis and helpdesk operations. This could also include education of subscribers.

Both technical and organizational measures have to be 'appropriate'. The second sentence of Article 4(1) states that, having regard to the state of the art and the cost of their implementation, these measures need to ensure a level of security appropriate to the risk presented. What is appropriate therefore depends on the seriousness of the risk involved, what kinds of measures are technically possible and available, and what it would cost to implement them. Appropriate is a discretionary notion. It will depend on the circumstances of each individual case what measures have to be taken.

As technical measures are further developed all the time it is impossible to lay down a minimum required level of protection in legislation. As for organizational measures, it seems reasonable for these measures to have a certain level before they gain any effect. For instance, educational material should be brought to the attention of subscribers and should be easily accessible. It is unclear how far a provider should stretch to inform its subscribers of possible risks involved. Relevant requirements can be put into legislation more easily than requirements for technical measures.

3.4   INTERPRETING THE NOTION OF 'SECURITY'

Apart from the question of who is responsible for security of the data, it is not clear what situations are covered by the reference in Recital 20 of the E-Privacy Directive to Article 17 Data Protection Directive. Several interpretations of Article 4 are possible in this light. A restrictive interpretation would lead to the conclusion that the duty to take measures only points to an obligation to protect those data the service provider processes himself. A broader interpretation would include the duty to protect against unsolicited or damaging information. The question is whether this includes hacking of servers which contain personal data databases (e.g., directories) and listening in on data-traffic in order to harvest e-mail addresses. In our opinion, it is reasonable to state that this is covered by the Directive.

Another interpretation of the notion of security could be significant with regard to anti-virus protection. The mass-mailing worm SOBIG.F marks a trend of spamming tools used in concert with computer worms.[86] SOBIG.F supposedly can also open up computer ports, making them vulnerable to hacking. Finally, the worm is said to spoof sender information and to use e-mail addresses that are harvested from the infected computer. The worm is believed to be used deliberately by spammers, to be able to use infected computers as open relays for more future spamming activities. The integration of spamming and virus communities is an enormous addition to the spam problem. In this interpretation of security, providers do have certain obligations with respect to prevention, also through means of education and notification, as well as damage control after the fact. However, in other matters than privacy, these issues seem questions to be answered by general liability law, which includes the duty of care for providers with regard to the security of their networks or services.

3.5   4(2): Duty to Inform

Article 4(2) of the E-Privacy Directive contains an obligation to inform customers about potential security breaches. Since spam can contain viruses, under certain circumstances spam can also be considered a 'breach of the security of the network'. This could mean that communications service providers have an obligation towards their users to warn them if there is such a spam attack and of what they can do about it themselves.

It is unclear whether the obligation to inform subscribers concerning such a risk includes an obligation of notification after the fact. However,

---

[86] 'Spreading SoBig. F Variant Fastest Outbreak Ever', *TechNewsWorld*, 21 August 2003. Available at <http://www.technewsworld.com/perl/story/31393.html>.

we assume that under certain circumstances the obligation of a service provider to inform his subscribers in case of a particular risk of a breach of security, also includes the risk following a breach of security that has already occurred.

3.6   CONCLUSIONS

In this chapter we described the specific section of the E-Privacy Directive dealing with network security. Article 4 introduces the obligation for providers to take appropriate measures in order to safeguard the security of their services. In case of a particular risk of a breach of security, the provider must also inform subscribers concerning such risk and of possible remedies available. A development with serious security implications is the convergence of spam and viruses.

The E-Privacy Directive addresses security issues and requires appropriate measures to be taken by providers. This does not introduce a strong right for users to object to their providers about letting through spam. Under certain circumstances, tort law or contract law could oblige providers to take measures against spam and viruses, such as filtering. A duty to act could be reasonable as soon as the access to either network or services is threatened due to spam and viruses. Service providers should inform their customers about their spam policy and possibly about available technological solutions.

Can a communications service provider hold the network service provider liable for not fully securing the network, as a result of which the communications service provider is facing a lawsuit from one his subscribers? The Directive does not answer that question but it cannot be excluded. In the end, it is a matter of national law whether liability of the service provider is inferred as a result of this part of the E-Privacy Directive.

Chapter 4
HARVESTING E-MAIL ADDRESSES

Chapter 4
HARVESTING E-MAIL ADDRESSES

4.1 INTRODUCTION

In order to send unsolicited communication a spammer needs personal data, such as e-mail addresses or phone numbers. Personal data can be collected by the marketer in several ways, not all of which are legitimate. They can be obtained directly from persons by request, they can be retrieved from a database which is compiled by another party, or they can be harvested on the internet. Databases may contain personal data that are collected in a legal manner, for instance by a business that went bankrupt and now sells the client database to pay its debts. Databases can also contain stolen personal data or personal data which have been harvested on the internet by means of a so-called 'crawler'. This is a computer program that roams the internet looking for electronic addresses, mostly e-mail addresses.[87]

In order to send unsolicited e-mail a spammer needs addresses. E-mail addresses can be collected by the marketer in several ways, not all of which are legitimate. They can be obtained directly from persons by request, they can be retrieved from a database which is compiled by another party, or they can be harvested on the internet. Databases may contain e-mail addresses that are collected in a legal manner, for instance by a business that went bankrupt and now sells the client database to pay its debts. Databases can also contain stolen addresses, or addresses which have been harvested on the internet by means of a so-called 'crawler'. This is a computer program that roams the internet looking for electronic addresses, mostly e-mail addresses.[88]

---

[87] A (web) crawler (also known as a 'web spider' or 'ant') is a program which browses the world wide web in a methodical, automated manner. Web crawlers are mainly used to create a copy of all the visited pages for later processing by a search engine, that will index the downloaded pages to provide fast searches. Wikipedia, available at <http://en.wikipedia.org/wiki/Main_Page>.

[88] Idem.

L.F. Asscher and S.A. Hoogcarspel, Regulating Spam
© 2006, T·M·C·ASSER PRESS, *The Hague, and the authors*

The Data Protection Directive contains rules on the processing of personal data. The Article 29 Working Party, the independent European advisory body on the protection of data and privacy, declared in 2000 the harvesting of e-mail addresses on the internet as amounting to unlawful processing of personal data according to the rules of the Data Protection Directive.[89] In this chapter, we will explain why this harvesting is contrary to Community legislation. We will discuss the relationship between the Data Protection Directive and the E-Privacy Directive and will try to determine if and how the Data Protection Directive offers additional protection to the E-Privacy Directive with regard to spam.

4.2   RELATIONSHIP BETWEEN THE DPD AND THE E-PRIVACY DIRECTIVE

According to Recital 10 of the E-Privacy Directive, the Data Protection Directive applies in parallel to the E-Privacy Directive. Recital 10 states:

Recital 10

In the electronic communications sector, Directive 95/46/EC applies in particular to all matters concerning protection of fundamental rights and freedoms, which are not specifically covered by the provisions of this Directive, including the obligations on the controller and the rights of individuals. Directive 95/46/EC applies to non-public communications services.

---

[89] Art. 29 Working Party 2000a, p. 77, confirmed by Art. 29 Working Party 2004, p. 6. The Art. 29 Working Party also has authority with regard to the E-Privacy Directive. Recital 48 of the E-Privacy Directive states: 'it is useful, in the field of application of this Directive, to draw on the experience of the Working Party on the Protection of Individuals with regard to the Processing of Personal Data composed of representatives of the supervisory authorities of the Member States, set up by Article 29 of Directive 95/46/EC'. Art. 15(3) of the E-Privacy Directive adds to this: 'The Working Party on the Protection of Individuals with regard to the Processing of Personal Data instituted by Article 29 of Directive 95/46/EC shall also carry out the tasks laid down in Article 30 of that Directive with regard to matters covered by this Directive, namely the protection of fundamental rights and freedoms and of legitimate interests in the electronic communications sector.'

This means that forms of processing personal data which are not covered by the E-Privacy Directive fall within the scope of the Data Protection Directive.

This is confirmed in Article 1 of the E-Privacy Directive, which states:

Article 1 'Scope and aim'

(1) This Directive harmonizes the provisions of the Member States required to ensure an equivalent level of protection of fundamental rights and freedoms, and in particular the right to privacy, with respect to the processing of personal data in the electronic communication sector and to ensure the free movement of such data and of electronic communication equipment and services in the Community.

(2) The provisions of this Directive particularize and complement Directive 95/46/EC for the purposes mentioned in paragraph 1. Moreover, they provide for protection of the legitimate interests of subscribers who are legal persons.

The phrase 'particularize and complement' in Article 1(2) of the E-Privacy Directive means that the Data Protection Directive provides for a general regime on data protection. The E-Privacy Directive offers a sector specific regime with regard to privacy and electronic communications. This means that only situations regarding processing of personal data, which are not covered by the E-Privacy Directive, fall within the scope of the Data Protection Directive. It also means that the E-Privacy Directive has to be interpreted in a manner consistent with the Data Protection Directive.

The second sentence of Article 1(2), on the protection of the legitimate interests of subscribers who are legal persons, is explained in Recital 12 of the E-Privacy Directive, which states:

Recital 12

Subscribers to a publicly available electronic communications service may be natural or legal persons. By supplementing Directive 95/46/EC, this Directive is aimed at protecting the funda-

> mental rights of natural persons and particularly their right to pri-
> vacy, as well as the legitimate interests of legal persons. This Di-
> rective does not entail an obligation for Member States to extend
> the application of Directive 95/46/EC to the protection of the le-
> gitimate interests of legal persons, which is ensured within the
> framework of the applicable Community and national legislation.

Although Member States have an obligation to protect the legitimate interests of legal persons, data related to legal persons are not personal data and
the rules of the Data Protection Directive do not apply.[90]

What provisions of the E-Privacy Directive may be of importance to our
subject? First of all, a special regime dedicated to the prevention of harvesting is provided for by Article 12 of the E-Privacy Directive on directories.
Article 12 obliges Member States to make sure a subscriber's permission is
obtained before being listed in a printed or electronic directory of subscribers (most importantly: the phonebook) available to the public through directory enquiry services and that they are informed about its purposes and
possible further usage.[91]

Secondly, as we have seen in chapter 3, Article 4 of the E-Privacy Directive provides, under circumstances, for a service and/or network provider
to take appropriate technical and organizational measures to safeguard security of is services and/or networks and for the duty to inform customers

---

[90] It is a matter of discussion in legal literature whether or not legal persons have a right
to privacy. If the scope of a right to privacy is limited to an personal and intimate sphere, is
seems hardly imaginable that a legal person should have a right to privacy. For other aspects
of privacy, such as confidentiality of communications and special privacy, this is less obvious. The ECHR has issued jurisprudence in which legal persons are granted a right to respect for the home, one of the aspects of privacy mentioned in Art. 8 of the European
Convention of Human Rights (*Chappell* v. *the United Kingdom*, Judgment of the ECHR 30
March 1989, Appn. No. 10461/83; *Niemietz* v. *Germany*, Judgment of the ECHR 16 December 1992, Appn. No. 1370/88; and especially *Stes Colas Est and others* v. *France*, Judgment
of the ECHR 16 April 2002, Appn. No. 37971/97. All available at <http://hudoc.echr.coe.int)>.
The European Court of Justice had earlier declined the possibility that legal persons
have a right to privacy (*Hoechst*, ECJ 21 September 1989, C-46/87 and 227/88), but recently seems to accept that legal persons have a certain right to privacy (*Roquette Frères SA*,
ECJ 22 October 2002, C-94/00).

[91] Art. 16 of the E-Privacy Directive states that Art. 12 does not apply to editions of
directories, which have been already produced or placed on the market in printed or off-line
form, before the national provisions which transpose the Directive enter into force.

about potential security breaches. Harvesting can be considered as such a security risk and network and/or service providers might have the obligation to secure their services and networks against harvesters.

4.3 PERSONAL DATA AND UNLAWFUL PROCESSING

Which electronic e-mail addresses can be classified as personal data and why is harvesting contrary to Community law? According to Article 2(a) of the general Data Protection Directive, 'personal data' means the following:

> **Article 2(a) DPD**
>
> 'personal data' shall mean any information relating to an identi-fied or identifiable natural person ('data subject'); an identifiable person is one who can be identified, directly or indirectly, in par-ticular by reference to an identification number or to one or more factors specific to his physical, physiological, mental, economic, cultural or social identity.

In the 1985 Recommendation of the Council of Europe on the protection of personal data used for the purposes of direct marketing, 'personal data' is defined as 'any information relating to an identified or identifiable indi-vidual (data subject). An individual shall not be regarded as "identifiable" if the identification requires an unreasonable amount of time, cost and man-power.'[92]

Direct identification means that an e-mail address contains one or more of the mentioned identifiable factors, such as a name, so that the person to which the data relate can be identified without the use of a third source. For example <name.surname@e-mailaddress.com>. One speaks of 'indirect identification' when identification of the person to which the data relates is possible without disproportionate efforts. It depends on the circumstances, *inter alia*, the way e-mail addresses are obtained, whether the e-mail ad-

---

[92] 1985 Recommendation of the Council of Europe on the protection of personal data used for the purposese of direct marketing, Appendix with Guidelines.

dress is personal data protected by one of the specific or general data protection Directives.[93]

Other examples of personal data are phone numbers and IP addresses. Phone numbers allow indirect identification of the subscriber through reverse directories as well as through telecom providers. Since a phone number is a personal item, which is tied to a telephony service by means of a personal contract, identification of the subscriber will often mean identification of the user. IP addresses allow indirect identification. IP addresses can be traced back to a computer, and through the internet service provider to a subscriber. Also dynamic IP addresses can be traced back to a computer. Although the link between subscriber and user is less strong compared to e-mail addresses and phone numbers, most IP addresses can be tied to a log-in and therefore may qualify as personal data.

Processing of personal data has to conform to the principles set out in the Data Protection Directive. Processing of personal data means, according to Article 2(b) of the Directive the following:

> **Article 2(b) DPD**
>
> 'Processing of personal data' ('processing') shall mean any operation or set of operations which is performed upon personal data, whether or not by automatic means, such as collection, recording, organization, storage, adaptation or alteration, retrieval, consultation, use, disclosure by transmission, dissemination or otherwise making available, alignment or combination, blocking, erasure or destruction.

The collection or harvesting of e-mail addresses obviously fits this definition.

The general rules with regard to the lawfulness of processing of personal data, can be found in Articles 6 and Article 7 of the Data Protection Directive. Article 6 describes the principles relating to data quality, Article 7 the criteria for making data processing legitimate.

---

[93] Lodder 2004, p. 73.

Article 6 DPD

(1) Member States shall provide that personal data must be:

(a) processed fairly and lawfully;
(b) collected for specified, explicit and legitimate purposes and not further processed in a way incompatible with those purposes. Further processing of data for historical, statistical or scientific purposes shall not be considered as incompatible provided that Member States provide appropriate safeguards;
(c) adequate, relevant and not excessive in relation to the purposes for which they are collected and/or further processed;
(d) accurate and, where necessary, kept up to date; every reasonable step must be taken to ensure that data which are inaccurate or incomplete, having regard to the purposes for which they were collected or for which they are further processed, are erased or rectified;
(e) kept in a form which permits identification of data subjects for no longer than is necessary for the purposes for which the data were collected or for which they are further processed. Member States shall lay down appropriate safeguards for personal data stored for longer periods for historical, statistical or scientific use.

(2) It shall be for the controller to ensure that paragraph 1 is complied with.

Article 7 DPD

Member States shall provide that personal data may be processed only if:
(a) the data subject has unambiguously given his consent; or
(b) processing is necessary for the performance of a contract to which the data subject is party or in order to take steps at the request of the data subject prior to entering into a contract; or
(c) processing is necessary for compliance with a legal obligation to which the controller is subject; or

> (d) processing is necessary in order to protect the vital interests of the data subject; or
>
> (e) processing is necessary for the performance of a task carried out in the public interest or in the exercise of official authority vested in the controller or in a third party to whom the data are disclosed; or
>
> (f) processing is necessary for the purposes of the legitimate interests pursued by the controller or by the third party or parties to whom the data are disclosed, except where such interests are overridden by the interests for fundamental rights and freedoms of the data subject which require protection under Article 1(1).

The most important principle of the Data Protection Directive is that the processing must be 'fair'. This means that the user of the electronic address (the data subject) must have been provided with certain information before he discloses his or her data and must have consented to the use to which it is to be put. The information to be provided to him includes the identity of the data controller, the purpose for which the data is to be processed and any further information which is necessary, having regard to the specific circumstances in which the data is or are to be processed, to enable processing in respect of the data subject to be fair.[94]

Article 2(h) of the Data Protection Directive provides for a definition of 'consent':

> **Article 2(h) DPD**
>
> the data subject's consent shall mean any freely given specific and informed indication of his wishes by which the data subject signifies his agreement to personal data relating to him being processed.[95]

The Article 29 Working Party is of the opinion that if an e-mail address is collected in a public space on the Internet, its use for unsolicited electronic

---

[94] Owen & Kiernan Earl 2003, p. 3.

[95] Art. 2(f) of the E-Privacy Directive subsequently states that consent by a user or subscriber corresponds to the data subjects' consent in the Data Protection Directive.

mailing would be contrary to the relevant Community legislation for three reasons. Firstly, it could be seen as 'unfair' processing of personal data under the terms of Article 6(1)(a) of the Data Protection Directive. Secondly, it would be contrary to the 'purpose principle' of Article 6(1)(b) of that Directive. When persons publish their e-mail address for a specific purpose, for example to participate in a newsgroup, this purpose is quite different to that of commercial e-mailing. Thirdly, given the cost imbalance and the nuisance to the recipient, such mailing could not be regarded as passing the balance of interest test in Article 7(f).[96]

In the *Lindqvist* case, the European Court of Justice clarified the application of the Data Protection Directive to the posting of personal information on Internet web sites.[97] The Court held that the act of referring, on an internet page, to various persons and identifying them by name or by other means (giving their telephone number or information about their working conditions and hobbies) constitutes 'the processing of personal data wholly or partly by automatic means'.

Furthermore, the Court discussed the question whether the posting of personal data on Internet Web sites could amount to the transferring of such data to a third country. Article 25 of the Directive prohibits the transfer of personal data to third countries that do not provide adequate protection to personal data, unless one of the (limited) exceptions apply. Given the state of development of the internet at the time the Directive was drawn up and the absence of criteria applicable to use of the internet, the Court takes the view that the Community legislature did not intend the expression 'transfer of data to a third country' to cover the loading of data onto an internet page even if such data are thereby made accessible to persons in third countries. Web site operators posting personal data on line are not subject to the legal regime pertaining to the transfer of personal data, unless they actually send the personal information to Internet users who did not intentionally seek access to web pages, or the server infrastructure is located on a non-EU country.

Also, certain software applications which use electronic addresses are subject to data protection rules. These so-called social applications such as Plaxon (automatic address book updater), Friendster and Hyves (extensions

---

[96] Art. 29 Working Party 2000a, p. 77.
[97] European Court of Jusitice 6 November 2003, Case C-101/01, *Bodil Lindqvist*.

of your social network), meetup.com. etc. use snowball techniques to verify and gather electronic addresses. These kinds of applications are based on the principle of exchanging electronic addresses with others, sometimes by means of a database which belongs to a third party. This kind of use is processing within the meaning of the Data Protection Directive and consequently, the principles on data processing apply.[98] This means that it is possible that those applications are not allowed under data protection law unless specific consent is acquired for those forms of processing. Those type of applications are a possible source for harvesters and must also be secured according to the principles on security of processing that can be found in Articles 4 of the E-Privacy Directive and Article 17 of the Data Protection Directive.[99]

4.4 DPD ENFORCEMENT

According to Article 28 of the Data Protection Directive, a public authority (the data protection authority) needs to be responsible for monitoring the application of the provisions adopted by the Member States. As provided for in Article 24, Member States need to adopt suitable measures to ensure the full implementation of the provisions of this Directive and shall in particular lay down the sanctions to be imposed in case of infringement of the provisions adopted pursuant to this Directive. Often this will result in an administrative fine.

According to Article 22 of the Data Protection Directive, without prejudice to any administrative remedy for which provision may be made, *inter alia*, before the supervisory authority referred to in Article 28, prior to referral to the judicial authority, Member States shall provide for the right of every person to a judicial remedy for any breach of the rights guaranteed to that person by the national law applicable to the processing in question. Member States shall provide that any person who has suffered damage as a result of an unlawful processing operation or of any act incompatible with the national provisions adopted pursuant to this Directive is entitled to re-

---

[98] Aoun & Rasie 2003

[99] For more on network security and the possible obligations and liabilities of service and/or network providers, see chapter 3.

ceive compensation from the controller for the damage suffered.[100] The controller may be exempted from this liability, in whole or in part, if he proves that he is not responsible for the event giving rise to the damage.[101]

4.5 CONCLUSIONS

Harvesting and scanning of old directories are forms of collecting and therefore processing of personal data, which can under certain circumstances be unlawful. To collect an electronic address in an electronic address book or to use this address to send a spam message also qualifies as processing of personal data. Processing of personal data has to be in accordance with the principles of the Data Protection Directive.

Moreover, the Article 29 Working Party also recalls that e-mail harvesting, i.e., the automatic collection of personal data on public Internet places, e.g., the web, chat rooms, etc., is unlawful under the 1995 Data Protection Directive 95/46/EC.[102] Notably, it constitutes unfair processing of personal

---

[100] Art. 23(1) DPD.

[101] Art. 23(2) DPD.

[102] Compare the Dutch case of *Netwise Publications BV* v. *NTS Computers Technology BV,* District Court Rotterdam, 5 December 2002, *Computerrecht 2003/2*, p. 149 in which a company called NTS had 'harvested' the addresses from the web site of Netwise. That web site contains a publicly accessible directory of e-mail addresses. Visitors to the web site can fill in their (e-mail) address on the site themselves. Anybody can search the directory by name and also, or alternatively, by place. At the same time Netwise had installed some technical security devices, providing a limit to the number of e-mail addresses that one can collect from the directory. Despite this, NTS had succeeded in collecting vast numbers of e-mail addresses from the directory, to which addresses they subsequently sent vast quantities of e-mail advertisements.

The Rotterdam District Court granted an injunction ordering NTS to stop collecting e-mail addresses from the Netwise directory. An important consideration was that all users of Netwise had been the guarantee that their data would not be used for spam. The general conditions of Netwise contain a full restriction on spam. In its defence NTS argued that that restriction was invalid because the general conditions had not been properly declared applicable, for nowhere on the web site were visitors specifically asked to confirm acceptance of the general conditions. However, the Court decided that in the circumstances such (confirmation of) acceptance was not necessary. It held that a professional visitor of web sites, like NTS, should be expected to understand that Netwise would attach such conditions – which the visitor can easily find and inspect – to the use of the directory. Furthermore, so the Court held, NTS should be expected to know that managers of e-mail files usually do not want 'harvesting' and spamming.

data and respects neither the purpose limitation principle, nor the obligation of information mentioned above or could it be regarded as passing the balance of interest test. This is also the case when automatic collection is performed by software.[103]

The E-Privacy Directive provides for a sector specific regime with regard to privacy and electronic communications. Only situations pertaining to the processing of personal data which are not covered by the E-Privacy Directive fall within the scope of the Data Protection Directive. In addition, the provisions of the E-Privacy Directive need to be interpreted in a manner consistent with the Data Protection Directive. The most important provisions of the E-Privacy Directive for our subject are Article 4 and Article 12. Article 4 provides for a possible obligation for a network/service provider to protect their networks and/or services against security risks such as harvesting and for the duty to inform customers about potential security breaches. Article 12 provides for the obligation to make sure a subscriber's permission is obtained before being listed in a printed or electronic directory of subscribers available to the public through directory enquiry services and that they are informed about its purposes and possible further usage. Hence, subscribers can prevent their personal data from being harvested from the directory.

It must be noted however, that for the subject of harvesting, the provisions of the Data Protection Directive are far more important.

---

[103] See also Recommendation 1/99 on Invisible and Automatic Processing of Personal Data on the Internet Performed by Software and Hardware, adopted by the Working Party on 23 February 1999, 5093/98/EN/final, WP 17.

Chapter 5
IMPLEMENTATION AND ENFORCEMENT

Chapter 5
IMPLEMENTATION AND ENFORCEMENT

5.1 INTRODUCTION

EU Member States were required to transpose the E-Privacy Directive by 30 October 2003, effectively replacing the ISDN Privacy Directive by that date. Nevertheless, only six countries had taken measures to transpose the Directive and infringement procedures where opened by the Commission against the remaining Member States for not adopting the new privacy rules for digital networks and services. At this moment, most Member States have adopted transposition measures. However, on the basis of concerns identified in the Commissions 10th implementation report on the electronic communications sector, the Commission launched infringement procedures against ten Member States for non-conformity with the E-Privacy Directive, and more in specific against Latvia, Malta and Slovakia and Austria for non-conformity with the rules on unsolicited communications.[104] The claims point to defects in national law and incorrect practical application of EU rules.

Ex Article 18, a review of the E-Privacy Directive by the Commission is foreseen 3 years after coming into force, i.e., not later than October 2006. This means that the Commission is monitoring national transposition measures ever since the implementation deadlines expired. In its 9th Implementation report of the telecommunications packages, the Commission stated that the E-Privacy Directive constitutes a vital element in the new framework and it therefore will carefully monitor whether its key concepts are properly transposed in national transposition measures.[105] The Commission also explicitly stated that, even though the Directive introduced an

---

[104] Press release, 'EU rules on electronic communications – Commission launches infringement proceedings against ten Member States', IP/05/430, Brussels 14 April 2005.

[105] 9th Implementation report, p. 39.

L.F. Asscher and S.A. Hoogcarspel, Regulating Spam
© 2006, T·M·C·ASSER PRESS, *The Hague, and the authors*

exception to the general opt-in rule for spam in Article 13(2) concerning direct marketing of a company's own similar products, if such an exception is transposed into national law, it should be strictly drawn up as not to undermine the general opt-in rule.[106]

Also, effective and timely enforcement is essential to ensure a real protection of subscribers. Therefore the Commission demanded that real and serious sanctions are introduced in the event of breach of the relevant rules. Those sanctions must include financial penalties where necessary. That implies that the responsible authorities must have the proper powers of investigation and enforcement.[107]

In this chapter, we will not provide a complete overview of implementation in all Member States, but rather focus on some interesting differences in approach. While by now, all Member States have implemented the Directive, the variety in implementation is large. We will pay attention to the implementation measures in France, Germany, the Netherlands and the United Kingdom.

It must be noted that, even where comparable ways of implementing have been chosen by Member States, the practical meaning of new laws can differ enormously because of differences in interpretation methods or differences in other national law aspects such as the division of the burden of proof.

In chapter 5.2, we will look at the national implementation measures taken. The protection of corporate interests, as provided for in Article 13(5) of the Directive, will be touched upon in chapter 5.3. To a great extent, the Directive leaves the question of enforcement up to the Member States. Chapter 5.4 discusses the national enforcement frameworks put in place by the several Member States. Both in choice of authority and in terms of choice of method of enforcement, serious differences appear between Member States.

As has been concluded already many times before, the importance of international co-operation needs to be stressed. Spam is a cross-border issue that requires international co-operation both in developing a common

---

[106] Ibid., p. 40.

[107] Idem. More on the implementation of the regulatory framework on electronic communications can be found at the Commissions Information Society Thematic Portal on e-communications <http://europa.eu.int/information_society/policy/ecomm>.

strategy and in enforcement. Efforts on international co-operation are touched upon in the next chapter.

5.2 NATIONAL IMPLEMENTATION MEASURES

5.2.1 **France**

Article 13 of the E-Privacy Directive has been implemented under French law by Article 22 of the '*Loi du 21 juin 2004 pour la confiance dans l'economie númerique*', [the Law on Confidence in the Digital Economy].[108] This law came into force on 22 June 2004. It amends the French Consumer Code and the French Code on Postal Services and Electronic Communications.[109]

Using the personal data of physical persons to send commercial e-mail without consent being obtained is prohibited, as well as sending or instigating the sending of commercial e-mail without indicating or while concealing their identity. In addition, marketers must also always provide a valid address to which the recipient can send an opt-out message. In the context of an existing business relationship, the sending of commercial e-mail marketing purposes is allowed without prior consent, when the personal data relating to the individual concerned has been collected directly from him or her in the context of a sale or service, the direct marketing is limited to similar products and services provided by the same individual or legal entity that obtained the individual's details and the individual was offered an opt-out when his or hers details were first obtained and each time a marketing e-mail is sent.[110]

Prior to the introduction of the above-mentioned provisions on spam, the use for purposes of direct marketing of automated calling machines without human intervention, including fax machines was already prohib-

---

[108] '*Loi no. 2004/575 du 21 juin 2004 pour la confiance dan l'economie numérique, JORF du 22 juin 2004*', p. 11168. Available at <http://www.legifrance.gouv.fr>.

[109] Art. 34-5 of the '*Code des postes et communications électronique*' and Art. 121-20-5 of the '*Code de la consommation*'.

[110] For more on the implementation of the E-Privacy Directive under French law see, *inter alia*, Penven & Wilhelm 2004 and Rojinsky & Teissonniere 2005.

ited, unless prior consent was given. Other techniques of distance communication were only allowed to be used where there was no clear objection
from the consumer.[111] In addition, the collection of e-mail addresses which
could considered to be personal data, relating to an identified or identifiable
natural person, and the use of these address without the consent of the data
subject or the data protection authority was and still is prohibited under the
'*Loi du 6 janvier 1978 relative a l'informatique, aux fichiers et aux libertés*'
[the Data Processing, Data Files and Individual Liberties Act 1978].[112] Until
22 December 2004, enterprises were allowed to use addresses lawfully obtained under the latter act to get the consent required under the new Law on
Confidence in the Digital Economy.

5.2.2 Germany

In Germany, the provisions on spam of the Directive have been incorporated into § 7 of the '*Gesetz gegen den unlauteren Wettbewerd*' [the Act
against Unfair Competition], which came into force in July 2004.[113]

A commercial e-mail sent without prior permission from the addressee
will constitute an unreasonable nuisance under competition law.[114] Where
the identity of the sender on behalf of whom the e-mail is being sent is
disguised or made secret, there will be an unreasonable nuisance as well. In
the context of an existing business relationship, similar provisions apply to
those described under French law above and mentioned in Article 13(2) of
the E-Privacy Directive.

The opt-in approach of the Directive is not new to German law. Before
the introduction of the statutory provisions specifically referring to spam,
on the basis of court decisions on general law, the sending of commercial e-
mail without prior consent was already in breach of competition law and an
interference with the legal interests of the recipient protected under tort

---

[111] French Consumer Code Art. L.121-20-5, inserted by Order No. 2001-741 of 23 August 2001 Art. 5 and Art. 12 *OJ* of 25 August 2001.

[112] '*Loi n° 78-17 du 6 Janvier 1978 relative à l'informatique, aux fichiers et aux libertés.*'

[113] '*Gesetz gegen den unlauteren Wetbewerb vom 3. Juli 2004*' (*BGBl.* I 2004, 32/1414).
Available at <http://bundesrecht.juris.de/bundesrecht/uwg_2004/index.html>.

[114] For more on the New Act on Unfair Competition and the provisions on spam, see
Finger & Schmieder 2004.

law.[115] If neither prior consent nor presumed agreement to the unsolicited commercial e-mail was given, the e-mail recipient had a claim for compensation under the Unfair Competition Act and the general tort law provisions of the German Civil Code by analogy owing to the interference in the general right of personality or in the business operation established and exercised.[116]

5.2.3   The Netherlands

Mainly by amending Article 11.7 of the '*Wet van 19 oktober 1998, houdende regels inzake de telecommunicatie*' [Telecommunications Act], the spam provisions of the Directive were implemented under Dutch law. The amendments entered into force on 19 May 2004.[117]

Sending electronic messages to subscribers for purposes of direct marketing, including non-commercial and charitable advertising, is not allowed unless prior consent is given. The burden of proving this prior consent is explicitly placed on the sender. These electronic messages must in all cases include information on the true identity of the entity sending marketing information, as well as a valid address to which a request not to receive future messages can be send.

The opt-out regime can be used in accordance with provisions similar to those described under French law above with regard to the context of an existing business relationship and mentioned in Article 13(2) of the E-Privacy Directive.[118]

---

[115] Funk, Zeifang, Johnson & Spessar III 2004, p. 138. See for example, *Bundesgerichtshof* 11 March 2004, I ZR 81/01 K&R 2004, 290 in which the court stated that the sending of commercial e-mails in not in contravention of competition law and thereby permissible only if the recipient has expressly or implicitly declared its prior consent to receive e-mail advertising or if an objective interest of the recipient can be presumed owning to specific actual circumstances in the case of advertising *vis-à-vis* businesses.

[116] Funk, Zeifang, Johnson & Spessar III 2004, p. 140. The e-mail recipient could bring an action to cease and desist or a claim for compensation pursuant to §§ 1 and 13 of the Old Unfair Competition Act and §§ 823(1) and 1004 of the German Civil Code.

[117] '*Wijziging van de Telecommunicatiewet en enkele andere wetten in verband met de implementatie van een nieuw Europees geharmoniseerd regelgevingskader voor elektronische communicatienetwerken en diensten en de nieuwe dienstenrichtlijn van de Commissie van de Europese Gemeenschappen*', *Staatsblad* 2004, 189.

[118] For more on the implementation of the E-Privacy Directive under Dutch law, see, *inter alia*, Thole 2004 and Lodder 2004.

Before the amendment of Article 11.7 of the Telecommunications Act, the same article provided that the use of automatic calling machines without human intervention and faxes for purposes of direct marketing, including non-commercial and charitable advertising, was not allowed unless prior consent was given. The use of other means for the purposes mentioned above was allowed, unless the recipient made use of the possibility to opt-out. The marketer was obliged to inform the recipient of this latter possibility. However, it was allowed to inform the recipient only once a year via a newspaper. There was no obligation to notify the recipient in every message.

5.2.4   The United Kingdom

In the UK, the provisions of the E-Privacy Directive were implemented under English law by the Privacy and Electronic Communications (EC Directive) Regulations 2003 S.I 2003/2426, which came into force on 11 December 2003. More specifically, Regulation 22 of these Regulations on E-Privacy introduces an opt-in regime for individual subscribers in relation to the sending of unsolicited communications by the means of electronic mail.

This Regulation provides that unsolicited communications for the purposes of direct marketing may not be transmitted, nor may transmission be instigated, unless the recipient has indicated that he does not object.

When the recipients contact details were obtained in the course of a sale or negotiations of a sale of a product or service to that recipient, when the direct marketing is in respect of similar products and services and there is a possibility to opt-out, companies may continue to market by means of electronic mail. As we have seen in chapter 2.6.2, the preparatory process of the E-Privacy Directive clearly indicates that there has to be a finalized contract for the soft-opt in rule to apply, and therefore in our opinion, the Directive was not implemented correctly under English law. In addition, the Information Commissioner's Office (ICO) takes a rather liberal view in a guidance issued.[119] According to the ICO, for the soft opt-in rule to apply, the sale does not have to be concluded yet. Where a person has actively

---

[119] ICO Guidance 2003. The ICO is the authority responsible for enforcing the Regulations.

expressed an interest in purchasing a company's products and services, and not opted out of further marketing of that product or service or similar products and services at the time his details were collected, the company may continue to market them by e-mail unless and until that person opts out of receiving such messages at a later date.[120] Even the collection of e-mail addressed or mobile phone numbers as part of a competition would be, under circumstances, considered as being in the course of negotiations for the sale of a product and services. As stated by the ICO, the intention of the section on 'similar products and services' is to ensure that an individual does not receive promotional material about products and services that they would not reasonably expect to receive. An individual who feels that the company has gone beyond the boundaries of their reasonable expectations, there is always a possibility to opt-out. The ICO states that it will only focus particular attention on failures to comply with the opt-out rules. This means that the soft opt-in approach pursued by the European legislator, in practice is not quite followed by the English enforcement authority. The way the ICO interprets the statutory provisions on E-Privacy, in our opinion results in an opt-out regime. On the other hand, the ICO states that it will continue to monitor the extent to which marketers take the reasonable expectations of individual subscribers about what falls within the phrase 'similar products and services' into consideration. The guidance is just a policy document and it is possible that the ICO will change its approach taken.

While the Regulations apply as of 11 December equally to data collected after that date, as to e-mail contact data collected before that date, the ICO is lenient again and takes the view that provided legacy data were obtained in accordance with privacy legislation enforced before 11 December 2003 and have been used recently, they can continued to be used on an opt-out basis. The Article 29 Working party takes a harder line in its Opinion on unsolicited communications. According to the Working Party, lists which have not been established according to prior consent requirement, may not be used any more under the opt-in regime.[121]

When implementing European legislation, the United Kingdom often takes a 'piecemeal' approach. The new rules are not incorporated into the existing legal frameworks, but a brand new Regulation is made to fulfill

---

[120] Ibid., p. 21.
[121] Art. 29 Working Party 2004, p. 6.

their obligations under European Law. Other provisions that apply to direct marketing by means of electronic communications can be found in the – rather extensive – Data Protection Act 1998 and the Electronic Commerce (E-Directive) Regulations 2002.[122]

5.3   POSITION LEGAL PERSONS

A very important area of diverge in implementing the Directive is the protection of corporate interests as provided for in Article 13(5) of the Directive. While this Article requires Member States to take measures in order to protect the interests of corporations, it is left up to Member States to decide whether legal persons and users that are not subscribers are protected by the opt-in rule of Article 13(1). This leaves Member States a wide margin of appreciation.

In most Member States, the opt-in rule does not apply to corporate subscribers. Article 11.8 of the Dutch Telecommunications Act explicitly states that Article 11.7 of that same Act is only applicable to subscribers that are natural persons. It must be noted, that this might change in the near future. The responsible Minister is preparing a legislative proposal that seeks to introduce an opt-in regime for corporate subscribers. Sending unsolicited communications to companies will still be allowed when a company makes available a special e-mail address for the purpose of receiving unsolicited communications and announces it as such.[123]

The English Regulations on spam provide for an opt-in regime for individual subscribers. Nevertheless, this does not mean that it does not apply to corporate subscribers in a broad sense. Because the Regulations define 'individual' as a living individual including an unincorporated body of such individuals, individual subscribers will also include sole traders and non-

---

[122] For an overview of the provisions that apply to direct marketing in the Data Protection Act 1998 and the Electronic Commerce Regulations as well as the new regime of the E-Privacy Regulations: Boardman 2004a and Donovan 2004.

[123] Letter from the Dutch Minister of Economic Affairs, Mr. L.J. Brinkhorst, to the Chairman of the Second Chamber of Parliament on his policy regards spam and the state of affairs in December 2004, *Kamerstukken 2004-2005, 26643, nr. 61, Tweede Kamer*.

limited liability partnerships, which are, in England and Wales, unincorporated bodies of individuals.[124]

The French laws on spam prohibit the use of personal data of physical persons to send commercial communications without consent. It therefore does not matter if you are a company subscriber or a private person; it depends on whether the e-mail address used to send the commercial communication is personal data of a physical person. For example, e-mail sent to the address <info@corporationx.com> is not protected by the opt-in regime, whereas the address <john.smith@corporationx.com> is.[125]

The German legislator did not choose to include less strict conditions for e-mail recipients who are not natural persons because of the fact that e-mail advertising in the business sector has a strong nuisance factor.[126] The provisions pertaining to spam apply irrespective of whether the recipient is a natural or a legal person, a consumer or a businessman. However, Germany is quicker to accept implied consent in the case of corporate users, than when private individuals are concerned.[127]

5.4 ENFORCEMENT

5.4.1 Introduction

In what way are the implemented provisions of the E-Privacy Directive enforced? When considering new legislation on any topic, it is relevant to take a look at enforcement mechanisms in place. In this chapter, we will make a few remarks on this difficult topic. Note that enforcement mechanisms are mainly a matter of national (Member State) law and that it is therefore not very useful to make far-reaching statements on pan-European enforcement. Enforcement can be hindered, *inter alia*, by a lack of cost effectiveness, by difficulties in tracking spammers, difficulties in collecting evidence and by differences in Regulation between Member States.

---

[124] Boardman 2004a, p. 16.

[125] The French authority responsible for enforcing these spam laws, the CNIL, stated in its annual report 2004 that it will re-examine the opt-in regime in the area of business to business marketing. CNIL, '*25e rapport d'activité 2004*', p. 67.

[126] A. Funk, G. Zeifang, D.T. Johnson, R. W. Spessar III 2004, p. 143.

[127] Boardman 2004c. Boardman refers to Regional Court of Berlin, *NJW* 1998, 3208.

Sometimes existing privacy legislation can also cause obstacles to effective law enforcement.

Recital 47 (of the E-Privacy Directive) urges Member States to provide for judicial remedies where the rights of users and subscribers are not respected. Recital 47 further states that penalties should be imposed on any person, whether governed by private or by public law, who fails to comply with the national measures taken under the E-Privacy Directive.

According to Article 15(2) the provisions of the Data Protection Directive on judicial remedies, liability and sanctions shall apply with regard to national provisions adopted pursuant to the E-Privacy Directive and with regard to the individual rights derived from this Directive. Article 15(3) states that the Article 29 Working Party on the Protection of Individuals with regard to the Processing of Personal Data, shall also carry out the tasks laid down in Article 30 of the Data Protection Directive applicable with regard to matters covered by the E-Privacy Directive, namely the protection of fundamental rights and freedoms of legitimate interests in the electronic communications sector.

Member States can choose to introduce penalties through civil, penal or administrative law. Because Recital 47 refers to 'judicial remedies', it will not be possible to rely solely on co-Regulation or self-Regulation. There has to be a final say by a court, be it a civil, penal or administrative court. Before turning to the different remedial options, we will first look at the differences in enforcement authorities.[128]

5.4.2   Enforcement authorities

Enforcement is not the responsibility of the same authority in all Member States. Because e-mail addresses that identify an individual are considered to be personal information to which data protection laws apply, in a majority of states, the data protection authority enforces the rules in the first place. In other countries, the national regulatory authority for electronic communications enforces the provisions on unsolicited communications. Sometimes more than one authority is involved in enforcing the provisions. In some instances, spamming also amounts to fraudulent or misleading prac-

---

[128] A lot of information about anti-spam law enforcement efforts worldwide can be found in the anti-spam law enforcement report of the OECD, OECD 2005.

tices. In this case consumer protection authorities would enforce the relevant rules. The principal reason for the plurality of enforcement agencies with responsibility for spam is that the variety of abuse committed through electronic communications may violate protections provided for under various laws – consumer protection law, criminal law, data protection law, telecommunication law –, each attributing responsibility to a different agency. In the following, we will focus our attention on the authorities responsible for the enforcement of anti-spam provisions enacted as a result of the need to implement the E-Privacy Directive as described above.

In France, the data protection authority *'Commission Nationale de l'informatique et des Libertés'* (CNIL), is responsible for enforcing the spam laws based on the Law on Confidence in the Digital Economy.[129] In order to ensure compliance, the CNIL may use in respect of the relevant provisions of the French consumer code and the French Code on Postal services and Electronic Communications its powers given under the Articles of the Data Processing, Data Files and Individual Liberties Act.

The English Regulations on E-Privacy are also enforced by the data protection authority, the Information Commissioner's Office (ICO).[130] Article 31 of the Regulations on E-Privacy extent the enforcement powers given under the Data Protection Act 1998 for the purpose of the Regulations.

In the Netherlands on the other hand, on the basis of Article 15.3 of the Telecommunications Act the national regulatory authority for electronic communications, the *'Onafhankelijke Post en Telecommunicatie Authoriteit'* (OPTA), has jurisdiction to supervise the compliance with the provisions on spam in the Telecommunications Act.[131] In cases were the Telecommunications Act is applicable, but because of the processing of personal data also data processing laws apply, there might be a concurrence of powers of OPTA and the Data Processing Authority, *'het College van Bescherming van Persoonsgegevens'* (CBP). To avoid problems, these authorities have concluded a co-operation protocol that gives OPTA the leading role in the fight against spammers in the Netherlands.[132] In respect of the enforcement of Article 11.7 of the Telecommunications Act, the protocol provides that,

---

[129] See <http://www.cnil.fr>.
[130] See <http://www.informationCommissioner.gov.uk>.
[131] See <http://www.opta.nl>.
[132] Samenwerkingsprotocol CBP-OPTA, 30 June 2005, *Staatscourant* 2005, 133, p. 27.

even though data protection laws apply, when electronic communications are used to transmit communication for commercial, ideal or charitable purposes, OPTA has jurisdiction and the CPB will leave enforcement matters up to OPTA.

In Germany, strangely enough no public agency is responsible for the enforcement of § 7 of the Act against Unfair Competition. Enforcement is left up to private parties that can bring suit under the law specified, such as direct competitors, consumer organizations, chambers of commerce and certain other associations. This topic will be discussed more in detail below.

5.4.3   Notification of complaints

The first step in the enforcement of spam laws involves receiving complaints about spam. In France the CNIL developed the idea of operation a 'Boite a spam' to receive complaints. This electronic mailbox was used to receive forwarded spam messages for the purpose of studying the problem of spam. While the messages where not treated as complaints but simply as a source of information, the CNIL did act upon receiving some of the forwarded spam messages. However, not very successful. The CNIL referred just five spammers to the public prosecutor who started criminal proceedings against them. Only one of them is convicted up till now. The spammer needs to pay a fine of 3000 Euro.[133] Nowadays, complaints to the CNIL can only be sent by mail. No actions taken by the CNIL upon receiving complaints are reported yet.

English recipients of spam who wish to make a complaint to the Information Commissioner about a breach of the Regulations on E-privacy must download and complete an Unsolicited Electronic Mail Complaints form from the ICO web site and submit this either by post or by mail. The Information Commissioner has received about 600 spam complaints from July 2004 to July 2005. But, the ICO has taken no legal action, in part because its powers are inadequate and impractical.[134]

---

[133] The spammer in question was La Societe Alliance Bureautique Service. Tribunal de Grande Instance Paris, 30 May 2005.

[134] Interview from OUT-LAW with Caroline Monk, Casework and Advice Manager with the ICO following the publication of ICO's annual report 2005 'UK Regulator Wants Power to Stop Spammers', 18 July 2005 <www.out-law.com>.

In the Netherlands, a complaint can be filed at a web site specifically designed for this purpose, <www.spamklacht.nl>.

Except in a few Member States, complaints do not necessarily have to lead to investigations. They often have discretion whether to investigate complaints. Authorities also often act on their own initiative. The resources of most authorities are limited, therefore different approached to handling complaints depending on the type of illegal activity at hand are used. There are still a lot of uncertainties about the rules on spam and legitimate businesses that have overlooked the law are often not pursued with the full powers of the authorities. In a lot of cases, authorities find that warning letters are sufficient.

5.4.4 Gathering evidence

One of the greatest challenges that enforcement authorities face is identifying the source of spam and gathering evidence to link a specific person to the act of sending spam. Therefore, authorities need tools to obtain sufficient evidence for investigations to proceed to the sanctioning phase of enforcement. It must however be noted that Article 8 ECHR on the right to respect private and family life provides that there shall be no interference by a public authority with the exercise of this right except such as is in accordance with the law and is necessary in a democratic society in the interests of national security, public safety or the economic well-being of the country, for the prevention of disorder or crime, for the protection of health or morals, or for the protection of the rights and freedoms of others. Hence, the authority to interfere with a spammers right to privacy, for example the authority to ask an ISP for information on the spammer or more compulsory means of obtaining information such as via subpoena or a court-ordered warrant, has to be provided for by law and be sufficiently exact.

Under Dutch law for example, Article 18.7 of the Telecommunications Act provides that, when reasonably necessary to exercise the enforcement powers given under the law, OPTA has the authority to demand inquiries from anyone. It is questionable whether this provision is sufficiently exact to fulfill the requirements of Article 8 ECHR.[135] OPTA feels that it is sufficient and that when investigating a breach of the provisions on spam it not

---

[135] See, *inter alia*, De Ru & Spaans 2004, p. 269.

only has the authority to ask for required personal data, but also that there is an obligation for those asked to co-operate.[136] If one does not co-operate, this might lead to the imposition of a fine by OPTA.

Not all authorities have compulsory powers to obtain information. In the UK for example, the ICO is authorized to approach a third party and ask for the identity of the sender, but may not compel them to provide information.

5.4.5   Initiating action; remedies and sanctions

The next step in enforcement is to initiate action. In general, three types of procedures may be used, namely administrative action, civil proceedings and criminal proceedings.

A variety of enforcement instruments are available in administrative law, such as issuing warning letters, orders to comply with the law and administrative fines. There are several advantages to acting trough administrative procedures.[137] When an authority is able to act on his own initiative, it does not have to rely on the discretion of a separate body such as the public prosecutor or consumer agencies to bring concrete action against spammers. Also, criminal and civil proceedings are often time consuming. In addition, criminal procedures may require a higher burden of proof, making it more difficult to obtain the remedy or sanction sought.

The cost-effectiveness argument is one of the reasons why criminal law is often regarded as the last resort in enforcing spam law. Hacking computers and/or domains to subsequently send spam runs from them is a criminal offence already in a number of Member States. The Convention on Cybercrime and the pending Council Framework Decision on Cyber crime also contain provisions regarding this kind of illegal activities.[138]

Penal sanctions can consist of punitive fines, a prison sentence and alternative sentences such as community work. It will depend on the penal system within the Member States what penalties are available and to what

---

[136] *Bekendmaking beleidsregels voor het vorderen van gegevens voor spamonderzoek*, *Staatscourant* 2005, 79, p. 25, available at <http://www.opta.nl/asp/besluiten/richtsnoeren/document.asp?id=1621>.

[137] See the Anti-Spam Law Enforcement Report of the OECD Task Force on Spam, 13 May 2005, p. 18.

[138] Convention on Cybercrim, Budapest 23 November 2001, entry into force 1 July 2004.

extent. This means that among those Member States that will choose penal law as a means to sanction spammers, big differences may arise in the severity of the sentences. Most member states punish spammers by imposing a fine. However, in Italy unlawful processing of personal data may be punished by imprisonment.[139]

Article 13(1) prohibits direct marketers from sending unsolicited e-mail to natural persons who did not give their prior consent. Because of the fact that this provision directly imposes obligations on individuals, this provision probably has horizontal direct effect, meaning that even when Member States have not implemented this provision into national law, subscribers can still bring a claim against the spammer under tort law as a breach of a legal requirement, asking for compensation. In all Member States, private individuals who suffer damages have an action in tort. The downsides of civil law actions are the costs, compared to the compensation the complainant will receive for one or a few e-mails sent by one spammer. The costs could be shared with other complainants by means of a class action or acting through means of an interest group.

Under French law, a breach of the provisions on spam is a violation of personal rights resulting from computer files or processes as defined by Articles 226-16 up to 226-24 of the Penal Code which may be sanctioned by a maximum of 5 years imprisonment and a 300.000 Euro fine. The CNIL has no authority to prosecute spammers under criminal law, but has the possibility to refer offenders to the public prosecutor who can start a criminal action. The CNIL can however apply one of the administrative sanctions within its powers, as for example to issue a warning which can be publicly diffused or ask the offender to stop sending illegal e-mails. If this does not have any effect, the CNIL can apply an administrative fine or use an injunction against the sender to stop his or her activity. If you do not respect the opt-in regime of the French Code on Postal Services and Electronic Communications, the CNIL may sanction you by a fine of 750 Euro per message. Even before the implementation of the E-Privacy Directive, the '*Tribunal de Grande Instance*' of Paris held that sending unsolicited bulk e-mail could be classified as criminal under French law.[140] Advertis-

---

[139] Boardman 2004b, part on Italy.

[140] *Tribunal de Grande Instance de Paris, 17ème chambre, No d'affaire*: 0205001163, 6 June 2003.

ing by electronic mail is subject to the Data Processing, Data Files and Individual Liberties Act, which protects individuals from the abuse of automated data processing and a violation of this act is under circumstances a criminal offence.[141]

The English authority ICO may take enforcement action on his own initiative or as a result of a complaint by a person affected or by the OFCOM, which is the independent regulator and competition authority for the UK communications industries, with responsibilities across television, radio, telecommunications and wireless communications services. Most of the spam complaints are dealt with by writing to senders. Clearly this does not always have effect and a lot of companies ignore the warning letters. The problem for the ICO is that the powers they have been given under the E-Privacy Regulations are not appropriate. The ICO has to supply a preliminary enforcement notice before it can issue a formal enforcement notice. An enforcement notice orders compliance where there has been a breach or an ongoing breach of the Act, which requires data controllers to take specific steps or to stop taking steps in order to comply with the law. A breach of an order is a criminal offence carrying a fine of up to £5000. The enforcement notice can be appealed at the Information Tribunal. The appeal costs nothing and most of the enforcement notices are appealed. Often, it takes very long for the Information Tribunal to convene and because of the fact that the ICO has no powers to stop the alleged spammer in the meantime, most companies are able to continue their unlawful activities.

In annual report 2004 of the ICO, Richard Thomas (the Information Commissioner) wrote 'Our experience in taking enforcement action in connection with unsolicited marketing faxes has convinced us that our existing enforcement powers are inappropriate. They do not allow us to take decisive action against those who continue to send unsolicited marketing material.'[142] Adding that 'The Department of Trade and Industry is committed to reviewing our existing powers and continues to explore the possibility of providing us with some form of injunctive power which will enable us to

---

[141] For information about the competences of the CNIL, see <www.cnil.fr>, 'approfondir', 'dossiers', 'spam'.

[142] The Information Commissioner Annual Reports and Accounts for the year ending 31 March 2004, p. 42.

take swift effective action'. However, no changes have been made up to now.[143]

On the basis of Article 30 of the Regulations on E-Privacy, individuals may seek compensation from the spammer if they have suffered damages by reason of a contravention of any of the requirements of the Regulations. Because of the fact that the individual needs to prove physical or economic loss for unsolicited communications, it is probably of limited application. A competitor that has complied with the Regulations may also have a remedy on the basis of the Regulations if it can show that it has lost sales to an organization that has not complied.

The Dutch OPTA has discretion to take administrative action in case of a breach of the Regulations on spam. Chapter 15 of the Telecommunications Act provides that OPTA has the authority to take enforcement measures, such as issuing orders to comply or administrative fines. Most of the times, OPTA will start by issuing a warning, but if the breach is sufficiently severe it will impose a fine. The amount depends on the gravity and length of the offence as well as due care taken by the spammer. In a policy document on imposing fines in the area of spam, OPTA states that is will sanction a breach with a maximum fine of 100.000 Euro per breach or in case of a very severe breach with a maximum fine of 450.000 Euro.[144]

OPTA is positive about its efforts to limit spam.[145] According to OPTA, the amount of spam coming from the Netherlands has decreased significantly. More than 7.000 complaints were filed, 21 warnings and 4 administrative fines of 2000 Euro up to 42.500 Euro were issued by OPTA.[146]

As mentioned above, in Germany, no public agency is responsible for the enforcement of § 7 of the Act against Unfair Competition. In § 8(3), the

---

[143] See the Information Commissioner's Annual Report 2004-2005, p. 15.

[144] '*Bijlage bij boetebeleidsregels OPTA: boetebeleid en handhavingsbeleid spam*', *Staatscourant* 2005, 145, p. 10.

[145] Press release, '*Resultaten eerste jaar spambestrijding positief*', 3 June 2005 <www.opta.nl>.

[146] For example, Stichting Yellow Monday was fined 20.000 Euro. Using the name 'Purple Friday' it sent sms-messages for commercial purposes without the legally required consent of the recipient. In addition, the recipients were charged for 1.10 Euro per received message. '*Besluit van 9 december 2004, zaaknummer JBOEO4002*'. See also '*Besluit van 23 december 2004, zaaknummer JBOEO4004*', '*Besluit van 23 december 2004, zaaknummer JBOEO4005*', '*Besluit van 19 mei 2005, zaaknummer JBOEO5001*'. All available at <www.opta.nl>.

parties that can bring suit under the law are specified. Organizations who can suit spammers are direct competitors, consumer associations, chambers of commerce and certain other associations. The civil remedies of the act are exclusive and consumers do not have standing. They have to complain to a consumer's association that can then bring a suit on behalf of the consumer. The most important organizations involved in spam are the 'ECO', the Association of the German Internet Economy and the 'VZBV', the Federation of German Consumer Associations.[147] January 2005, a legislative proposal with regard to amending § 7 of *'Das Gesetz uber die Nutzung von Telediensten'* [the Telecommunications Act], has been submitted to parliament. The proposal seeks to introduce a prohibition to send commercial communications by electronic mail without indicating its commercial character and the concealment or falsification of the identity of the sender. Upon breach, a fine up to 50.000 Euro may be issued.

The e-mail recipient has a claim in tort against the sender to a cease and desist order and to compensation under §§832 (1) and 1004 of the German Civil Code by analogy owing to interference in the general right of personality or in an established and existing business.

5.4.6 Execution

Once there is a court ruling, this ruling has to be executed. There are European and international treaties on recognition and enforcement of judgment. However, there are a number of countries that do not participate in execution treaties so even when the spammer is identified and tried before a court, it might be difficult to execute the ruling of that court. Therefore, co-operation with the countries from which a lot of spammers originate, e.g., the United States, is necessary.[148] The next chapter deals with the efforts to co-operate internationally and the challenges to cross-border enforcement more in detail.

---

[147] See <http://www.eco.de> and <http://www.vzbv.de>.
[148] According to Spamhaus, the United States is the worst spam originating country <http://www.spamhaus.org/statistics/countries.lasso> (last visited 26 September 2005).

5.5 CONCLUSION

In order to have a serious impact on the actual proliferation of spam, a lot depends on how the new Regulations are implemented into national law. Most Member States have now fully implemented the Directive. This chapter deals with national implementation measures taken. While most Member States chose to implement the required provisions in their data protection laws, other Member States amended their consumer codes, telecommunications codes or their competition laws. Once again, the UK made a brand new statutory instrument to fulfill their obligations under EU law.

Member States have used the full margin they are allowed to choose their own implementation of the E-Privacy Directive. Large differences exist between individual Member States in terms of scope of protection they decided to offer users as well as in terms of the position of legal persons. For example, whereas in the UK for the soft opt-in rule of Article 13(2) E-Privacy Directive to apply, the sale does not have to be concluded yet, in the Netherlands this is a prerequisite. In general, the UK is less strict than the other Member States discussed when it comes to the opt-in regime. Under German law, the opt-in rule applies whether the recipient is a natural person or not, in the Netherlands the opt-in rule only applies to subscribers that are natural persons. In France it depends on whether personal data of physical persons is used to send the commercial communication, in the UK unincorporated bodies of living individuals are protected by the opt-in regime and other corporate subscribers are not.

The choice of enforcement methods has been left largely up to individual Member States, which in effect means that very different systems have been put in place. Issues like complaints mechanisms, choice of public or administrative law and penalties are dealt with in altogether different ways in a lot of EU Countries. The Commission seems to have realized that this development could threaten the practical effect of the Directive and has stressed the importance of effective enforcement mechanisms in its 2004 Communication. The choice of sanctions to be used against violations of the anti-spam laws also presents significant differences. Not all authorities have appropriate powers to stop spammers quickly.

Linked to the question of which enforcement mechanism is adopted, is the question of who will be responsible for enforcement. The E-Privacy Directive does not specify which authority should be in charge of enforcing

spam laws. This means that it is left up to the Member States to decide
whether they leave it up to their Data Protection Authorities, like in France
and the United Kingdom, or their National Regulatory Authorities, like in
the Netherlands. It is even possible to leave this responsibility with a general consumer protection authority like the Swedish Consumer Ombudsman. In Germany, there is no authority at all to enforce the implemented
provisions and enforcement is left up to private parties. The E-Privacy Directive only imposes obligations to implement material provisions on spam.
However, we feel that the German solution regards enforcement might be
not what the Commission had in mind. It is questionable whether without a
public enforcement authority, it could be said that real protection of subscribers is ensured. Hopefully, this will change in the near future.

The powers given to the responsible authorities, in our opinion, do not
have much effect on spammers yet. So far, not much cases of successful
action against spammers are reported, but for in the Netherlands. Most authorities just issue warning letters, which is obviously not enough for the
majority of spammers. A big problem for enforcement authorities seems to
be the identification of the source of spam and the gathering of evidence to
build a case against a spammer. However, it must be noted that while the
fight against spam is important, so is the right to respect private and family
life.

Even when good and effective legislation is implemented in one country, it cannot stop unsolicited e-mail coming from other countries. To effectively fight the spam problem, enforcement agencies need to co-operate
with foreign counterparts in taking action against spammers. The next chapter
deals with the challenges to effective cross-border enforcement and the international initiatives in the field of spam.

In our opinion, because of the differences in national implementation
measures taken, combined with the fact that enforcement is not harmonized
at all, the anti-spam framework put into place is rather confusing. Spam is
clearly a cross-border issue, but for a recipient in one Member State, it is
hard to find out what he can do about spam originating in another Member
States. To which enforcement authority should he turn? Or is there no enforcement authority to turn to at all, like in Germany? What remedies does
he have? Is the spammer facing imprisonment, a fine or just a warning?
When he receives the spam on a corporate account, is he still protected? On
the other side of the coin, it is hard for legitimate marketers to know what is

legitimate and Pan-European campaigns are difficult to start. They can be acting legitimately in one country and illicitly in the other.

The fact that the European Union pays a lot of attention to the spam problem and because of this, all Member States have adopted anti-spam legislation should be applauded. However, it should not be forgotten that we are not quite there yet. There are too many diverges in implementation methods to be effective on a pan-European level and a harmonized enforcement framework should be adopted too.

Chapter 6
INTERNATIONAL CO-OPERATION AND CHALLENGES TO EFFECTIVE CROSS-BORDER ENFORCEMENT

Chapter 6
INTERNATIONAL CO-OPERATION AND CHALLENGES TO EFFECTIVE CROSS-BORDER ENFORCEMENT

6.1 INTRODUCTION

The provisions of the E-Privacy Directive apply to all processing of personal data in connection with the provision of publicly available electronic communications services in public communications networks in the EU. All communications sent from or received on a public network within the EU are covered by the provisions on spam. Messages originating outside the EU must also comply with the rules.

A lot of spam originates from outside the EU, mostly from America, Africa or Asia. To enforce European anti-spam legislation outside the EU is problematic for a number of reasons. Also the enforcement of national legislation in which the European rules are transposed on an intra-European level may be difficult.

An enforcement authority that wishes to take action against a spammer located in a foreign country is often limited by the fact that it cannot exercise its full enforcement powers beyond national borders. To ensure effective protection against spam for their national recipients, authorities need to seek assistance from their foreign counterpart in the country where the spammer is located. They need to be able to locate and identify a foreign spammer and collect evidence against him to build a case. Therefore, co-operation in gathering and sharing information is needed. It must be noted however, that national data protection laws often restrict the voluntarily sharing of personal data between authorities. International co-operation in this area may not be in conflict with principles of data protection law. Also, the actual enforcement of the rules may be difficult because of jurisdic-

L.F. Asscher and S.A. Hoogcarspel, Regulating Spam
© 2006, T·M·C·ASSER PRESS, *The Hague, and the authors*

tional barriers and barriers as to recognition and enforcement of judgments and requires co-operation on an international level.

Due to its inherent international character, spam can only be fought effectively if countries co-operate. In the past few years, a number of international initiatives have been taken to tackle the spam problem. Besides the promotion of the adoption of effective legislation and common standards in countries that do not have them yet, the main objective of these global initiatives is to encourage countries to co-operate with each other to ensure effective enforcement of applicable rules.

In this chapter, the initiatives to improve co-operation within the EU are discussed in chapter 6.2. Chapter 6.3 elaborates on the most important initiatives on the international level, in particular touching upon their goals, objectives and achieved results. Some other aspects of cross-border enforcement, such as jurisdiction, applicable law and execution of the penalties are dealt with in chapter 6.4.

6.2   European Co-operation Initiatives

As provided for in Article 3(1) of the E-Privacy Directive, the Directive applies to the processing of personal data in connection with the provision of publicly available electronic communications services in public communications networks in the Community. This means that the opt-in regime applies to all unsolicited commercial communications received on and sent from networks in the EU (and EEA). Hence, messages originating in third countries must also comply with the EU rules, as must messages originating in the EU and sent to addressees in third countries.

In our opinion, on the basis of the Directive enforcement authorities also have jurisdiction to take enforcement action against foreign-sourced spam. All unsolicited commercial communications received on and sent from networks in the EU must comply with the rules. It does not matter where the spammer is located. However, the majority of Member States do not provide for this possibility in respect of intra-EU spamming or do not take action against them in practice, due to the difficulty of investigating and problems linked to the execution of an eventual judgment. In most Member States, enforcement action can be pursued by authorities against foreign spammers as long as the spammer is situated outside the EU, while spammers in the EU should be dealt with according to the domestic law in the message's country of origin.[149] Actual enforcement of the rules with regard to messages originating in third countries will clearly be more complicated than for messages from inside the EU. Because of Regulation (EC) No. 44/2001 of 22 December 2000 on jurisdiction and the recognition and enforcement of judgments in civil and commercial matters it is easier to try and enforce penalties on European offenders, that to pursue offenders from outside the EU.[150] It must be noted however, that this Regulation only applies to civil and commercial matters, and enforcement authorities enforcing administrative or penal law, do not benefit from it. The level of difficulty of enforcing penalties on offenders from outside the EU depends, *inter alia*, on what treaties regarding cross-border enforcement exist, and on the co-operation of nations involved.

In its Communication 2004, the Commission recognized effective law enforcement as one of the most important elements in the fight against spam, and still one of its weakest. The Commission stated that it is very important to ensure that the national complaint mechanisms, whatever their modalities, can be linked to ensure that complaints from users in one Member State regarding messages originating in another will be dealt with effectively.[151] The Dutch presidency of the Council of Europe considered the issue of spam as a priory issue in the internet security field and stressed the need for improved international co-operation too.[152] In reaction to this presidency paper, the Council adopted Conclusions on unsolicited communications for direct marketing purposes.[153] In these Conclusions, the Council also stressed the importance of improving co-operation on enforcement, information exchange and consumer protection at the intra-EU level.

The Commission tries to facilitate and promote co-ordination among competent national authorities through an informal on-line group on unsolicited commercial communications. To improve co-operation and discuss co-ordinated approaches to enforcement, at the initiative of the Commis-

---

[149] OECD 2005, p. 21.

[150] *OJ* L 012, 16.01.2001, pp. 1-23. For EU Member States except Denmark, this Regulation replaces the 1968 Brussels Convention on jurisdiction and the enforcement of judgments in civil and commercial matters and the analogous 1988 Lugano Convention.

[151] Communication 2004, p. 17.

[152] Presidency Paper 2004.

[153] Council Conclusions 2004.

sion the Directorate General Information Society assembled an informal group of National Authorities involved with the enforcement of Article 13 of the E-Privacy Directive called 'the Contact Network of Spam Authorities (CNSA)'.[154] The two enforcement authorities heading this group, the CNIL and OPTA, have circulated a questionnaire to other enforcement authorities in the EU, asking about implementation of the Directive, scope of the national rules and enforcement authorities and – mechanisms.[155] In the CNSA, information on current practices is exchanges between National Authorities, including best practices for receiving and handling complaint information and intelligence and investigating and countering spam.

Also, in a joint action of the CNIL and OPTA a co-operation protocol that aims to facilitate the transmission of complaint information or other relevant intelligence between National Authorities has been agreed upon in December 2004.[156] This voluntary agreement establishes a common procedure for handling cross-border complaints on spam. Parties to the agreement undertake to make their 'best efforts', as to close loopholes on spammers. On the basis of the agreement, when a National Authority receives complaint information and intelligence, it should do its best efforts to verify the possible grounds for involvement of other National authori-

---

[154] See Press release, 'European countries launch joint drive to combat spam', 7 February 2005, IP/05/146.

[155] The CNIL is the French data protection authority, the *Commission Nationale de l'Informatique et des Libertés*, and is responsible for enforcing the implemented provisions on spam of the E-Privacy Directive. OPTA is the Dutch national regulatory authority for electronic communications, *Onafhankelijke Post en Telecommunicatie Authoriteit*, and has the same responsibility under Dutch law. For more on these enforcement authorities, see chapter 5.4.

[156] Co-operation Procedure 2004. National agencies which have already agreed to use the procedure include Austria's Federal Ministry for Transport, Innovation and Technology, Belgium's Privacy Commission and Federal Public Service Economy – Directorate General Enforcement and Mediation, the Cyprus Office of the Commissioner for Personal Data Protection, the Czech Republic's Data Protection Authority, the Danish Consumer Ombudsman, the French data protection authority CNIL, the Hellenic Data Protection Authority, Ireland's Department of Communications, Marine and Natural Resources and the Office of the Data Protection Commissioner, Italy's Data Protection Authority, Lithuania's State Data Protection Inspectorate, Malta's Office of the Commissioner for Data Protection, the Netherlands' regulatory authority for electronic communications (OPTA) and Data Protection Authority (CBP), and the Spanish Data Protection Authority. See Press release, 'European countries launch joint drive to combat spam', 7 February 2005, IP/05/146.

ties. When another National Authority is competent to take action against the spam violation, the complaint information or intelligence is transmitted to the other National Authority, which deals with the claim. However, the agreement explicitly states that this transmission needs to be permitted by national law. As mentioned above, national data protection laws often restrict the voluntarily sharing of personal data between authorities.[157]

Much spam comes from outside the EU, and the Commission is aware of the fact that co-operation with third countries is necessary to be able to enforce the rules also against spammers from outside the EU. According to the Commission, obstacles to effective cross-border enforcement include the difficulty of identifying the senders of spam or the amount of effort required to do so, the lack of appropriate international co-operation mechanisms and the lack of jurisdiction of some authorities on international matters.[158]

Therefore, the Commission is active in international fora, most importantly in the context of the United Nations World Summit on the Information Society (WSIS) in which the ITU takes the lead role in preparations, and the OECD task force on spam, which will be both explained more in detail in the next chapter. In addition, it encourages Member States to engage in bilateral co-operation with third countries, not only for the protection of effective legislation, but also for co-operation on enforcement, including police and judicial co-operation, where appropriate.[159]

Other initiatives on an EU level, be it not particularly addressed to the spam problem, may be of importance to our subject too. In may 2005, the Council adopted the Safer Internet Plus programme, which aims to empower parents and teachers with better internet safety tools and to combat illegal and harmful internet content.[160] It establishes a multi-annual Community Programme on promoting safer use of the Internet and new on-line

---

[157] While these legal restrictions pertaining to data protection obviously do not facilitate effective cross-border enforcement, one should not forget that the right to respect private and family live is an important human right protected by, *inter alia*, Art. 8 ECHR. See also chapter 5.4.4.

[158] Communication 2004, p. 19.

[159] Communication 2004, pp. 19-20.

[160] Decision 854/2005/EC of the European Parliament and the Council of Ministers of 11 May 2004, 'Internet 2005-2008 action programme on promoting a safer us, Safer Internet Plus', *OJ* L 149, 11.6.2005, pp. 1-13.

technologies. The new programme also explicitly addresses the fight against spam. On the basis of this decision, funding will be available for developing better filter and promoting exchanges of information and best practices on anti-spam enforcement. The programme needs to be implemented by the Commission, but no concrete programmes or proposals have yet been adopted.

In the field of consumer protection, in October 2004 the European Parliament and the Council adopted a (non-spam specific) Regulation on consumer protection co-operation establishing a network of consumer protection authorities to deal with cross-border problems.[161] The Regulation puts in place mutual assistance procedures for operational co-operation between national authorities. The provisions of the Regulation only apply to intra-communautary infringements of laws that protect consumers' interests as defined in the Annex. Even though the E-Privacy Directive is not mentioned in the Annex and therefore cross-border enforcement of its provisions on spam is not facilitated by this Regulation, spam that is misleading or deceptive may be in breach of mentioned consumer protection laws.

6.3   INTERNATIONAL CO-OPERATION INITIATIVES

At an international level, the work on spam has been put high on the agenda. This chapter aims to highlight the most interesting initiatives.

In the context of the World Summit on the Information Society (WSIS) the problem of spam has been discussed thoroughly at a UN level.[162] The WSIS is held in two phases and the ITU takes the leading role in preparations. The first phase took place in Geneva in December 2003 with the objective to develop and foster a clear statement of political will and take concrete steps to establish the foundations for an Information Society for all, reflecting the different interests in stake. This resulted in a Declaration of Principles, setting out the key principles for building such an inclusive

---

[161] Regulation 2006/2004/EC of the European Parliament and the Council of 27 October 2004 on co-operation between national authorities responsible for the enforcement of consumer protection laws (the Regulation on consumer protection co-operation). *OJ* L 364, 9.12.2004, pp. 1-11.

[162] See also <http://www.itu.int/wsis/index.html>.

information society.[163] In this Declaration, it was recognized that spam is a significant and growing problem for users, networks and the Internet as a whole and that spam and cyber-security should be dealt with at appropriate national and international levels.[164]

The ITU also prepared an Action Plan, that aims to translate the common vision and guiding principles of the Declaration into concrete action lines.[165] When it comes to possible solutions to the spam problem, the Action Plan is rather disappointing. It states that 'confidence and security are among the main pillars of the information society' and that one of the action lines is to 'take appropriate action on spam at national and international levels'.[166] However, no more substantial actions to combat spam can be found in the Action Plan.

During the preparatory process for the second phase that will take place in November 2005 in Tunis, thematic meetings were held, *inter alia*, a thematic meeting on countering spam and on cyber security. These meetings discussed the spam problem and possible solutions from different perspectives and were attended by participants representing a range of government policy makers and regulators, international and intergovernmental organizations, privacy groups, representatives of communications service providers and ICT companies, academics, civil society organization and other interest groups.[167]

Another international organization that has started to work on spam is the Organisation for Economic Co-operation and Development (OECD). The aim of the OECD is to bring together all the actors in this field and fostering international co-operation. For this purpose, OECD members set up a 'Task Force to Coordinate Fight Against Spam', which started working in Autumn 2004. The Task Force has a policy oriented objective. It tries to co-ordinate international policy responses in the fight against spam, to encourage best practices in industry and business, to promote enhanced technical measures to combat spam along with improved awareness and

---

[163] WSIS Declaration of Principles 2003.
[164] Ibid., para. 37.
[165] WSIS Action Plan 2003.
[166] Ibid., para. 12.
[167] Background papers, presentations and other interesting information on spam can be found at the web site of the ITU on activities on countering spam <http://www.itu.int/osg/spu/spam>.

understanding among consumers and to facilitate cross-border enforcement. To achieve these goals, the Task Force has published an 'Anti-spam toolkit' to provide policy orientation and support. It is a policy document and a source of information and best practices for OECD as well as non-OECD members and is under constant evaluation.[168] For example, the toolkit includes an Anti-spam Law Enforcement Report which elaborates on the nature and extent of the powers possessed by agencies with responsibility for enforcing laws used to take action against and aims to provide for a basis for discussion on how to improve the capacity of enforcement agencies to respond to spam complaints and to co-operate with foreign counterparts.[169] Furthermore, in co-operation with the ITU, the Task Force compiled a list of competent enforcement authorities and their contact details.[170]

Several countries and organizations are taking action to improve international co-operation between enforcement authorities by entering into multilateral or bilateral memorandums of understanding (MoU), in particular with countries known to be sources of spam.[171] Basically, these MoU pertain to the co-operation in detecting and investigating spam violations,

---

[168] See ITU Task Force on Spam Toolkit 2005. The Toolkit is composed of 8 elements addressing regulatory and policy issues, technical solutions, enforcement concerns, and it includes education and awareness tools, suggestions for improved cross-border co-operation, industry driven initiatives and outreach activities. See also <http://www.oecd.org/sti/spam/toolkit>.

[169] Task Force on Spam, Anti-Spam Law Enforcement Report, 13 May 2005, JT00184175, prepared by the Directorate for Science, Technology and Industry, Committee on Consumer Policy and the Committee for Information, Computer and Communications Policy.

[170] This list is available at the OECD Work on Spam web site, at <http://www.oecd.org/sti/spam/>. See also the database on anti-spam laws and authorities worldwide, for which the content was gathered by the ITU in co-operation with OECD <http://www.itu.int/osg/spu/spam/law.htm>.

[171] For example, the Australian Competition and Consumer Commission, the Australian Communications Authority, the United Kingdom's Information Commissioner, the Office of Fair Trading in the United Kingdom, Her Majesty's Secretary of State of Trade and Industry in the United Kingdom and the US Federal Trade Commission MoU on mutual assistance in commercial e-mail matters of July 2004; Another example is the Seoul-Melbourne Anti-Spam Agreements between the Australian Communication Authority and the National Office for Information and Economy of Australia and the Korean Information Security Agency of October 2003. In April 2005 twelve other Asian-Pacific participants joined this MoU. For more examples of multilateral and bilateral co-operation, see the site of the ITU on international co-operation <http://www.itu.int/osg/spu/spam/intcoop.html>

the sharing of information and evidence between enforcement agencies and the promotion of anti-spam efforts in general on a national and international level.[172] These MoU are not legally binding, and co-operation pursuant to these MoU is subject to the laws and international obligations of participating countries and agencies. Most of the MoU recognize that the sharing of information between authorities may be privacy sensitive and that enforcement agencies should keep in mind to maintain the confidentiality of any information communicated to other participants and to disclose information only in accordance with privacy laws.

6.4   OTHER ASPECTS OF CROSS-BORDER ENFORCEMENT

While there are some international initiatives to co-operate in cross-border enforcement matters, when it comes to jurisdiction, applicable law and the execution of penalties in general one has to look at national laws on cross-border enforcement, i.e., private international law. Private international law is national law, even though it partly derives from international or European treaties.

In case of cross-border law enforcement, it must first be established in which country a case can be brought to court, before the applicable law or the way of executing the penalty can be assessed. Jurisdiction is derived from national rules of private international law, or from applicable international or European treaties. Both treaties and national legislation have exceptions on the general rules for certain kinds of cases, such as tort law or contract law cases.

---

[172] Most MoU on this subject are concluded between enforcement authorities, but the London Action Plan on Spam (LAP), agreed upon in October 2004 is a non-binding agreement open to signature by enforcement authorities, but also to certain private sector actors with an interest in combating spam. LAP members includes enforcement authorities from different jurisdictions and some key industry signatories such as ISP associations. The participants undertake to use their best efforts to develop better international spam enforcement co-operation, for example by the designation of a national point of contact for communication on spam cases with foreign authorities and by taking part in periodic conference calls to discus cases, legislative and law enforcement developments, exchanging effective investigation techniques and enforcement strategies. For more information and a list of signatories, see <www.londonactionplan.com> and the site of the ITU on international co-operation <http://www.itu.int/osg/spu/spam/intcoop.html>.

In general, a case must be brought before a court of the country of residence of the defendant. In the case of tort law, European jurisprudence states that also the court of the place where the damaging fact has occurred can decide on the matter. The place where the damaging fact has occurred can be either the place where the action was initiated (i.e., where the spam run was sent from) or the place where the result of that action occurs.[173] In the case of international spam runs, this could be anywhere in the world. To ground jurisdiction on the country of origin of the spammer could prove problematic, since spammers can locate themselves in spam harbors with no execution or extradition treaties. And even when a country is a party to such treaties, spammers can still move to certain areas within this country where these treaties are more difficult to enforce.

Jurisdiction which is based on the place of origin of the action is also problematic because it is very easy to put the server from which the spam run is sent in a spam harbor. This leaves the possibility to fix jurisdiction on the place where the result of the action occurs. This means that every country where a spam run has effect can designate a court before which a case against the spammer in question can be tried.

Jurisdiction based on the place where the results of the action occur would be very disadvantageous to E-marketers who wish to send legitimate mail. As long as they limit their marketing campaign to their own country they can probably figure out the relevant rules. However, if they operate internationally it will be hard to find out what is allowed where. Also, with some e-mail addresses like .com, .net or .org e-marketers cannot always establish for certain in which country the recipient is located. Permission marketers should then ask for more than just an e-mail address before they send out mail to potential customers. This will diminish the amount of addresses they will gather, because people do not bother, or do not want, to give out detailed information about themselves.

Once it has been established before which court a case can be tried, that court has to decide what law is applicable and therefore what kind of rules regarding spam apply. Some countries accept a choice of law by contract between civil parties. If an address is acquired in the context of a sale (as referred to in Art. 13(2) of the E-Privacy Directive) and the customer opted

---

[173] *Handelskwekerij G.J. Bier BV* v. *Mines de potasse d'Alsace SA*, Judgment of the ECJ 30 November 1976, case C-21/76.

out, but nevertheless receives e-mail from this company, the choice of law of the contract could also apply to unsolicited e-mail. If no choice of law has been made, the principle of *lex protectionis* may apply. This means that if a case is tried before a court of the country in which the results of the action have taken place, the court can apply the law of this same country. In the case of a spam run, this could mean that a spammer could be tried by a court of a foreign country, under foreign law. If the results of the action did not take place in the same country as that of the court trying the case, the court may use the 'contacts approach' to establish the applicable law. In that case, the law that is most closely connected to the matter has to be applied.[174] This connection can be established for instance by a previous customer relation. It would then depend on the circumstances of that relation which law would apply. The court can also apply the principle of the *lex loci delicti*, the law of the place where the action took place. In that case, it foreseeable that it will be hard to find out for an e-marketer what laws may apply to his actions.

For e-marketeers it is problematic to start Pan-European, let alone global campaigns. There are still so many different rules that apply to spam and they do not only have to comply with the rules of the country of establishment or the country out of which the spam is sent, but possibly also with those of the country of receipt. Even on a European level, due to the differences in implementation measures, it is complicated to understand the applicable rules.

6.5   CONCLUSIONS

While it is important to act at a national level, any spam-measures should always be considered at the international level. The internet knows no frontiers; spammer and message recipient are often located in different countries and enforcement authorities are therefore confronted with numerous challenges in their efforts to take legal action against a spammer.

In the past few years, a number of international and intergovernmental initiatives have been undertaken to control the spam problem. These initiatives seek to promote the adoption of effective legislation and common

---

[174] Trzakowski 2003, p. 5.

standards in countries that do not have them and to encourage countries to co-operate with others to ensure effective enforcement of the applicable rules.

At the EU level, first of all the E-Privacy Directive ensured that all Member States adopted anti-spam legislation. To improve effective enforcement of these provisions on spam co-ordination among the responsible authorities is facilitated and promoted through an informal on-line group and in the context of the CNSA. The recently concluded co-operation protocol has established a common procedure for handling cross-border complaints on spam. While this is a promising development, its effects should not be over-estimated. Nowhere near all of the responsible authorities have joined this agreement, and compliance is voluntary. In addition, the transmission of intelligence – which is one of the most important challenges to effective cross-border enforcement – may be difficult because of national data protection laws. On the other hand, because of the EEX Regulation on recognition and enforcement, once a private person has obtained a judgment against a spammer falling within the scope of this Regulation, it is much easier to effectively enforce this judgment inside the EU, than outside. The need for a more harmonized approach to intra European enforcement of the E-Privacy Directive, has already been stressed in the previous chapter.

At the international level, the momentum is definitely there. Policy makers have identified spam as a critical and global issue that requires co-ordination. Most importantly, the ITU and OECD are very active in this field. They have produced numerous documents explaining and analyzing the spam-problem and facilitating the exchange of information about existing practices to promote international spam enforcement co-operation. These policy documents all agree on the fact that a multi-faceted approach is the best way to combat spam. Effective spam law is needed in all countries, but also important are effective enforcement by the responsible authorities, cross-border co-operation on enforcement, technical and self-regulatory solutions by the industry to manage or reduce spam and greater consumer awareness about the subject.

Even though policy makers have produced a mountain of policy documents, in our opinion, so far no substantial steps to fight spam are really made. Most importantly, a well-co-ordinated, multilateral international framework is still lacking. Too many initiatives are discussed in too many fora. In addition, a more multilateral approach is needed. Bilateral and multilateral Memorandums of Understanding seek to improve international co-operation at the technical or regulatory level, fostering the exchange of information and best practices and promoting a co-operative approach to the problem. However, these initiatives should no longer be initiated bilaterally per country, but multilateral. Especially at an EU-level. A lot of Member States have concluded bilateral agreements with spam-originating countries, but the EU as an institution is the adequate forum to initiate a more co-operative policy and conclude global agreements as a Union.

Chapter 7
OTHER ASPECTS OF THE FIGHT AGAINST SPAM

Chapter 7
OTHER ASPECTS OF THE FIGHT AGAINST SPAM

7.1 INTRODUCTION

In this chapter we briefly describe a number of measures that are being taken against spam or that could be taken against spam and we assess their legal consequences. The question we try to answer in this chapter is: what are the alternatives to Article 13 of the E-Privacy Directive both technically and legally?

7.1.1 Anti-spam technology

Anti-spam solutions protect and help business, ISPs and individual users to reduce the amount of time spent reading and managing unwanted e-mail by filtering out inappropriate and offensive content. One of the options is the use of filters using 'blacklists', which consist of domain names or Internet protocol (IP) addresses of known spammers. Blacklists can be established in a collective way. Once enough recipients in a certain user community object to a particular message, the message is automatically transferred to future users' spam folders. Another technical option, consisting of 'white list', or 'approved sender lists', allows users to identify e-mail from approved and legitimate senders. While white lists can help refine spam filtering, they are currently prone to spoofing, or falsification of e-mail source data. Another technical tool which has been suggested as having good anti-spam potential is to set one's e-mail client to accept only messages signed with trusted digital certificates issued by a trusted certificate authority. Digital signature schemes such as public key infrastructure solutions can be used for this purpose.

L.F. Asscher and S.A. Hoogcarspel, Regulating Spam
© 2006, T·M·C·ASSER PRESS, *The Hague, and the authors*

7.1.2 Filtering

There are numerous technical approaches to try and stop spam, such as filtering and blocking of e-mail, distributed denial of service attacks or tracing a spam run to find and sue the spammer.

The majority of spam-blocking technologies currently use keyword or blacklist blocking, which results in a large number of false positives. False positives occur when a legitimate e-mail is mislabeled as spam and filtered. In addition, anti-spam blacklists sometimes block innocent Internet users connected through blocked ISPs. There have even been cases of entire country domains being blocked. While some users have felt empowered by these filters, many ISPs argue that they have had the effect of blaming the wrong people, including ISPs that host spammers unknowingly, Internet users who may have been spoofed by a spammer, and addresses adjacent to the alleged spammer.

Another approach to spam filtering is the consensus model, whereby people who receive messages that they consider to be spam report them as spam to a co-ordinating entity. A computer program is then used to co-ordinate all of the input. A properly compiled list of known spammers would also be a significant improvement on unregulated blacklists that currently operate. Nevertheless, perfect filter systems are nearly impossible to deliver.

Many spammers are technologically sophisticated enough to cover their tracks, adjust their systems to slip through filters and scale other technological barriers. They can electronically commandeer unprotected computers, turning them into a tool for their own spamming. As long as spam costs are so low, spammers have a vested interest in finding ways to defy technological limits.

Filtering is used in this study as a generic term for all kinds of technical features that aim to keep inboxes free from spam. Those technical measures can operate at mail server level or at inbox level. Blocking is a form of filtering at mail server level that does not allow the e-mail to go into the inbox of the individual user. Blocking e-mail is possible in at least two ways: through the use of black-lists and the use of white lists. Black lists block all e-mail coming from specific IP-addresses. They can also block whole servers. Another way to block e-mail is through the use of a white list. A disadvantage of using a white list is that the person who uses such a list cannot be reached by a person whom he did not add to the list. This inconvenience can be tackled by using an additional challenge response filter. When such a filter is used people who are not on the white list but wish to send e-mail to this user anyway, fill out a request form on a web page and then are added to the white list. This is convenient to the user, but inconvenient to the people who want to contact this user.[175] Also, some people use different (reply) addresses and have to make sure all those different addresses get white listed.

The downsides to blacklisting are clear as well. First of all, a lot of spam passes the filter that is supposed to block it. It is estimated that filters using blacklists only block 25 to 50 per cent of spam.[176] A weak spot of blacklisting is that it requires human intervention. Unless a domain that is being used by a spammer, is placed on the list, the spam will not be blocked. And since spammers continuously use different domains a lot of spam makes it through the barricades. A second disadvantage of using blacklists is that a lot of legitimate mail is being bounced.

A famous black list is the Realtime Blackhole List (RBL) of the anti-spam group MAPS (Mail Abuse Prevention System). The RBL is a blacklist of servers that are not anti-spam. ISP's can use this list to block e-mail from the servers on the list. However, the question whether an ISP has an active anti-spam policy or not is prone to debate. Aside from that, the RBL of MAPS is based on a definition of spam that takes a double opt-in system as a criterion for legitimate mail. This leaves out e-mail send by permission marketers which use single opt-in or opt-out schemes, sometimes according to the law of the country they originate from, or according to the law of the country they target. All e-mail from an ISP that is not anti-spam is blocked.[177]

Human intervention renders blacklists also susceptible to fraud. What is easier than having a competitor's domain put on a black list. It is an efficient way to rob people of their ability to communicate and therefore works as a means of obstruction of freedom of expression.[178] However, a respon-

---

[175] Graham 2003, p. 3.
[176] Graham 2003, p. 1, Graham 2002a, p. 1.
[177] Magee 2003, p. 25.
[178] Ibid., p. 6.

sible and actively kept up to date blacklist might be useful in combination with other ways to fight spam.[179]

Another problem with blocking mail at mail server level is that ISP's may under certain circumstances have an obligation to deliver e-mail sent through their services. This can be a contractual obligation towards their subscribers to send and deliver mail, or an obligation prescribed by law. In case of a contractual obligation, spam which is sent through the network of the provider can be excluded from this obligation by contract. Subscribers who still want to send or receive spam can go to an ISP with a more tolerant policy regarding spam.

Aside from blocking, there are numerous other forms of filtering. Graham presents an elaborate description of different ways to fight spam in 'Stopping Spam'.[180] The best known filtering techniques are rule-based (or heuristic) filtering and Bayesian (or statistical) filtering. While at first these were competing systems, nowadays they are used complementing each other.

Rule-based filters look for specific spam patterns in the text (header and body) of the e-mail, words such as 'cash', phrases like 'try for free!' and malformed headers are give always for the e-mail likely to be spam. Likely, because although a good heuristic filter can stop 90-95 per cent of spam, it can also refuse up to 5 per cent of legitimate mail. Also, since spammers use different patterns all the time, the programs of rule-based filters have to be rewritten constantly, resulting in expensive updates of anti-spam software. However, since rule-based filters can operate at mail server level, individual users do not necessarily have to switch to new version themselves all the time. However, the subscribers might still pay for the costs ISP's make on their behalf. Bayesian filters also look at words used in e-mails. Bayesian filters compare two lists, a list of legitimate e-mail and a spam list, that are kept by the user, and, based on those lists, add a probability for words to be used in spam or legitimate e-mail. Bayesian filters, if operated in the right way, can filter over 99 per cent of spam with a very low percentage of false positives. Bayesian filters learn through time and therefore work better the longer they are used, if both lists are being kept up to date. That is also the weak spot of Bayesian filtering, they require maintenance and are much harder, though not impossible, to operate at mail

---

[179] Graham 2003, p. 1.
[180] Graham 2003.

server level by an ISP.[181] Another negative aspect of Bayesian filters is the fact that they tend to lack in accuracy and that they cannot filter text which is put into GIF files.

Some anti-spam software uses a combination of filtering techniques to combat spam.[182] This will keep out the average spammer, but will not be sufficient to scare off the most technologically proficient spammers. Filtering will therefore in itself in all likelihood not eliminate the spam problem, but merely contain it.[183]

In our opinion, ISP's should let their subscribers decide whether they want their e-mail to be filtered or not, and in what way. Even, if it is necessary to filter e-mail (also) at mail server level, subscribers should be made aware of this and of the possible results of the kind of filtering that is used, such as the blocking of mail altogether or the filing of suspicious e-mails in a spam folder. In this manner e-mail users stay in control of their communications. Therefore users should have the option of using custom-made instead of ready made filters. ISP's should provide users with friendly software, or information on it, and help out with the settings of this software at user level since the ISP's benefit from a reduction of spam just as much. Ideally users can define what is spam to them, not someone on the server level only ISP's also filter e-mail for viruses. As the overlap between spam and virus mail grows, education and information on the uses of virus filters gets more important.

7.2   LEGAL ALTERNATIVES: TORT

As spam poses substantial costs, especially to ISP's, some American providers have sought to protect their interest by suing spammers for trespass to chattels and they have sought injunctive relief to protect their property.[184]

---

[181] Ibid., pp. 2-3.

[182] The free open software program SpamAsassin uses a variety of techniques to filter spam: header analysis, text analysis, blacklists and signature-based filtering. See <http://au2.spamassassin.org/index.html>.

[183] Magee 2003, p. 25.

[184] One of the first cases in which a court upheld and action for trespass to chattels in the spam context was *Compuserve, Inc.* v. *Cyber Promotions, Inc.*, 962 F. Supp. 1015 (S.D Ohio 1997). The district court found an ISP could claim trespass to chattels where a spammer had

Trespass to chattels is an action in tort based on the unauthorized use or interference with another's property. For the claim to be upheld, there must be some kind of damage, debilitation or removal of that property. But does this rule make sense in a virtual world with intangible property? In American case law, the foremost problem had been that trespass to chattel necessarily had to do with interference with or use of tangible property of another. In the context of spam, trespass to chattels occurs when the spamming interferes with the possessory interest of another through unauthorized use of their computer network. In addition, for the claim to be actionable, a plaintiff must have incurred 'actual injury' as a result of the spammer's interference.[185]

Some authors warn that side effects of allowing for an action in trespass to chattels, could prove detrimental to commons on the web. The endpoint to such a theory may be that a rights of use theory could develop that would scare anybody away who tries to reach an audience through internet.[186]

---

sent unsolicited commercial e-mail, even after being advised that certain recipients did not want to receive these messages. The court held that trespass to chattels included unauthorized use of personal property and that Compuserve was indeed harmed by losing customers who were upset by the amount of spam they were receiving and that the high volume of unsolicited commercial e-mail was preventing Compuserve's customers from having full access to the services they were paying Compuserve to provide.

[185] In *Intel Corp* v. *Hamidi*, 71 P.3d 296, 302-4 (Cal. 2003), the Court took a rather restrictive view on the applicability of a remedy in trespass to chattels. 'After reviewing the decisions analyzing unauthorized electronic contact with computer systems as potential trespasses to chattels, we conclude that under California law the tort does not encompass, and should not be extended to encompass, an electronic communication that neither damages the recipient, computer system nor impairs its functioning. Such an electronic communication does not constitute an actionable trespass to personal property, i.e., the computer system, because it does not interfere with the possessor's use or possession of, or any other legally protected interest in, the personal property itself. The consequential economic damage Intel claims to have suffered, i.e., loss of productivity caused by employees reading and reacting to Hamidi's messages and company efforts to block the messages, is not an injury to the company's interest in its computers – which worked as intended and were unharmed by the communications – any more than the personal distress caused by reading an unpleasant letter would be an injury to the recipient's mailbox, or the loss of privacy caused by an intrusive telephone call would be an injury to the recipient's telephone equipment.' This judgment make it harder for plaintiffs to have an action in trespass to chattels. See also Kam 2004. Other actions under Common Law that can be used by 'spam-victims', are for example breach of contract, trademark dilution and false designation of origin.

[186] Burke 1998, p. 31.

In its decision of 12 March, 2004, the Dutch Supreme Court upheld a tort based claim, much like trespass to chattels, of an ISP to refuse spam on its network.[187] According to the Supreme Court, the ISP had an exclusive property right to its network and the fact that the spammer used that network for sending out unsolicited communications amounted to an unlawful act towards the provider. Of course tort law differs largely between Member States, but the case could be followed by similar cases in other Member States, based on the claim that providers have an exclusive right to their networks and can therefore prevent unauthorized use of those systems.

The mirror image of the right of ISP's to refuse spam traffic is the possibility of a legal obligation for ISP's to filter out spam. In chapter 3, we have discussed the obligation of network and service providers to take appropriate measures in order to safeguard the security of their network and services. Under certain circumstances, it is conceivable that an end user may hold his ISP liable for not taking appropriate measures to protect him from unsolicited communications.

Another, more pragmatic approach to the spam problem could be to go after the vendors that profit from spam. If for example legitimate businesses see an increase of sales as a result of unsolicited communications it seems fair that they should be required to prove that they were not aware of the illegal advertising campaign and otherwise should be held liable for the damage inflicted on both ISP's and end users.

7.3   FRAUD AND DECEPTION

Fraudulent or deceptive spam can be targeted by criminal law. Fraud of a more serious kind is also very common in spam. Nigerian spammers pose a notorious example as they have stolen millions of dollars from people which believed their claims. In this 'Nigerian scam', the message originator wants to share million of dollars with the message recipient, but needs a down payment in advance. Of course, investment on return is zero. According to the OECD Background Paper, the US Secret Service has designated this type of spam scam as an 'epidemic' and claims that losses amount to hun-

---

[187] *Xs4all* v. *Abfab,* Supreme Court of the Netherlands, 12 March 2004.

dreds of millions of dollars annually.[188] Several kinds of pyramid schemes and 'get rich fast' tricks are floating in mailboxes and most phenomenal diet or body improvement advertisements seem as misleading as anything. Even more serious are the various kinds of illicit or illegal spam messages that promote prostitution, illegal on-line gambling services, drugs or weapons sales, and so forth.

7.4   Unsolicited Pornographic or Racist E-mail

A special category of spam content to be discussed here is Unsolicited Pornographic E-mail (UPE). Spam messages containing pornographic photographs, and promoting adult entertainment products and services are deemed inappropriate for children. Since many spammers do not target specific recipients, young children are likely to be inadvertently exposed to pornographic or offensive messages.[189] But aside from children, employees could have a right to be protected against pornographic e-mail in their workplace.

Under US Law, it is clear that pornographic e-mail leaves companies vulnerable to charges of creating a 'hostile work environment,' and all the associated liabilities that implies. Already, employers have been found directly and indirectly liable under these rules for failure to protect their employees from offensive imagery, and failing to monitor and prevent inappropriate use of e-mail when notified by employees of the problem.[190]

It is conceivable that European employers could also be held liable for not protecting their employees against unsolicited pornographic or racist spam. In Europe, employers have an obligation to protect their employees from discrimination in the workplace.[191] The concept of employment discrimination is expanding up to a level where the possibility of sexual ha-

---

[188] OECD 2004, pp. 15-16.

[189] Ibid., p. 16.

[190] Compare for example *Blakey* v. *Continental Airlines, Inc.*, Supreme Court of New Jersey, 164 NJ 38; 751 A.2d 538 (2000).

[191] See Council Directive 76/207/EEC of 9 February 1976 on the implementation of the principle of equal treatment for men and women as regards access to employment, vocational training and promotion, and working conditions, *OJ* L 039, 14.02.1976, p. 40, amended by Directive 2002/73/EC of the European Parliament and of the Council of 23 September 2002, *OJ* L 269, 5.10.2002.

rassment could also amount to employer liability for unsolicited porno-graphic e-mail.[192] Employers may also be vicariously liable for e-mail mis-use by their employees, including spamming.

7.5   SELF-/CO-REGULATION

There are a variety of ongoing self-regulatory efforts in place to reduce spam, see for example the European Code of Practice for the Use of Per-sonal Data in Direct Marketing of the Federation of European Direct Mar-keting (FEDMA). Even though a self-regulatory approach may contribute considerably to the fight against spam, a number of restrictions are clear. First of all, self-regulation will by definition mainly address organized or official direct marketers. 'Bad Spammers' will not follow rules of self-regu-lation and will therefore break through any protection against spam offered by self-regulation. It remains very easy for those bad spammers to use false identities, ever changing locations and new techniques to avert filtering software.

7.6   CONSUMER AWARENESS

The European commission explicitly pays attention to consumer education and awareness as an important step to decrease spam.[193] Increasing aware-ness of users of the risk of leaving e-mail addresses on numerous web sites is indeed a first step to prevent address harvesting. At the same time, that would make it harder and more costly for spammers to obtain those ad-dresses. Plus, the effects of consumer awareness are not limited to spam coming from Member States of the European Union. If people are more careful about their e-mail addresses, this would also give them a certain protection against spammers from third countries. The Commission has developed the so-called Safer Internet Action Plan to promote awareness-raising activities in Member States for the safe use of the Internet.[194]

---

[192] Waddington & Hendriks 2002.
[193] Communication 2004, pp. 25-28.
[194] See also chapter 6.2.

7.7   Conclusions

In this chapter, we have discussed a number of other aspects that are relevant in the attempts to regulate spam. First of all we paid some attention to
technological measures that can be taken against spam. Anti-spam technology offers practical protection against at least a large quantity of spam messages. However, we have also pointed out the inherent risks of trusting
technology to solve this problem. Both false positives – unjustly blocked
messages – and false negatives – spam messages slipping through – can
cause serious problems. It is important that users of anti-spam technology
are aware of those inherent risks in order to prevent the damage which can
be caused by important messages being blocked without justification.

Once again it is interesting to look at the specific responsibility of the
Internet Service Provider. Technical solutions can be implemented either at
the user level or at higher levels in the network. Employers often offer
spam filtering on their corporations' networks. For users which are natural
persons the most likely provider of filtering services however would be
their ISP. It is for a large part a matter of contract law between user and ISP
whether any obligation could exist to filter spam (except for possible obligations under the security provision of the E-Privacy Directive as discussed
in chapter 3).

Besides technological solutions, we briefly discussed some legal alternatives outside the present spam regulation that is the core subject of our
research. The property based claim of trespass to chattel, to be brought by
network owners has proven successful in some anti-spam cases both in the
US and in a similar way in the EU. Also, some spam may be targeted by
criminal law for being deceptive and fraudulent. The infamous example of
the Nigerian scammers proves that outside the electronic communications
framework, classic criminal law still applies to this kind of offences committed through sending unsolicited communications.

A specific remark has been made about the position of employers when
it comes to spam. We have argued that it is important that employers are
aware of potential risks of liability arising out of their failure to protect
employees from unsolicited pornographic e-mail. In the US, it has been
argued that failing to protect employees against these kinds of messages
could contribute to a hostile work environment. European law suggests that
the same reasoning could apply in a European context. Apart from binding

legal rules, some see a complementing role for self- or co-regulation. We do not believe that self-regulation will be the panacea to all spam problems, mostly because self-regulation does not tend to bind 'bad spammers'. Finally, the importance of consumer awareness has been stressed by the European Commission. We think that this is indeed an important aspect because lack of consumer awareness makes it very easy for spammers to keep collecting fresh and working e-mail addresses.

Chapter 8
CONCLUSIONS AND RECOMMENDATIONS

Chapter 8
CONCLUSIONS AND RECOMMENDATIONS

8.1   MAIN CONCLUSIONS

We have seen that spam poses a very complex problem to internet users, regulators and businesses. Therefore the solution to spam is not likely to be a simple one. A one-size-fits-all approach is not going to solve it.

The complexity of the spam issue is governed by its international dimension, the various opposite (fundamental right) interests of the actors involved, the lack of a single clear definition of spam and the present inadequacy of technological solutions.

The fight against spam represents a collision of the fundamental rights of spammer, recipients of spam and providers. We have called this clash of fundamental rights the spam triangle, because the relationship between spammer, provider and user can be seen as a triangular one, with the provider in the middle. On the one hand, we have seen that, although commercial communication in principle is protected by freedom of speech, freedom of speech does not grant the spammer a very strong claim against either provider or recipient. On the other hand, however, the recipient can claim both infringements on his relational privacy and on his informational privacy. The provider can claim ownership rights.

Informational privacy is protected by data protection law. It has been argued that the collecting via harvesting on the Internet and use of e-mail addresses without the users' consent would amount to an infringement on the Data Protection Directive. Even though it is hard to make a general statement on the legality of the collecting and use of e-mail addresses for spam purposes, it seems clear that large scale harvesting does amount to an infringement of at least some rights of data protection of users.

The 2003 E-Privacy Directive tries to contribute to an effective solution to the spam problem by regulating unsolicited communications for direct marketing purposes. It can be seen as an important first step in the fight

L.F. Asscher and S.A. Hoogcarspel, Regulating Spam
© 2006, T·M·C·ASSER PRESS, The Hague, and the authors

against spam. The EU has chosen a pan European opt-in rule as the norm throughout the EU. Although it remains to be seen how effective this opt-in regime will be in practice, it is clear that the pan European approach will have an important symbolic meaning in the international fight against spam. It is the first international norm with regard to spam. As such it will be the point of departure for spam initiatives on other forums. Next to that, the EU's initiative will be an important signal to all actors involved in the spam issue: the spammers, those who use spammers to advertise their goods or services, providers and Internet users.

In this report we have analyzed the object and scope of Article 13 of the E-Privacy Directive. We have seen that the opt-in rule in Article 13(1) could in theory have a broad applicability, because of the open definition of e-mail. Article 13(1) applies to users being natural persons in their capacity of subscribers. We have seen that outside that scope there is a possibility to choose between opt-in and opt-out for Member States. Article 13(2) introduces the possibility for continued direct marketing to existing customers for similar products. We have established that the wording of that second section leaves room for a myriad of interpretations.

Article 13(3) of the E-Privacy Directive provides protection in respect of the rest category. Unsolicited communications for direct marketing purposes that are not covered by the first two sections are covered by this section. This means that some of the newer forms of unsolicited communications such as pop-ups and SPIM are covered by this section and that Member States are under the obligation to provide some sort of protection against those unsolicited communication by choosing either an opt-in or an opt-out regime. Article 13(5) obliges Member States to provide protection for the legitimate interests of subscribers which are not natural persons.

We have seen that the meaning of this discrepancy between Article 13(1) and Article 13(5) will in practice largely depend on the national law division of the burden of proof. If the spammer carries the burden of proof to provide evidence that the recipient is not a natural person that would render it very risky to keep sending spam to corporate users also.

The practice of sending e-mails with false return addresses or using disguised or false identities is explicitly targeted in Article 13(4). That section requires Member States to prohibit the practice of sending electronic mail for purposes of direct marketing disguising or concealing the identity of the sender on whose behalf the communication is made, or without a valid address to which the recipient may send a request that such communications cease.

An important limitation on the effectiveness of the E-Privacy Directive on spam is the simple fact that most spam originates from outside the EU. Although the opt-in regime applies to all unsolicited commercial communication received and sent from networks in the EU, and hence, messages originating in third countries must also comply with the EU rules, in practice to enforce European anti-spam legislation outside the EU is problematic. Due to its inherent international character, spam can only be fought effectively if countries co-operate. In the past few years, a number of international initiatives have been taken to tackle the spam problem. The momentum is definitely there. Policy makers have identified spam as a critical and global issue that requires co-operation. Most importantly, the ITU and OECD are very active in this field. There is agreement about the fact that a multifaceted approach is the best way to combat spam. However, besides the numerous policy documents produced by policy makers around the world, in our opinion, so far no substantial steps to fight spam are really made. Too many initiatives are discussed on too many fora and a more multilateral approach is needed. Several Member States have concluded bilateral agreement with spam-originating countries, but the EU as an institution is the adequate forum to initiate a more co-operative policy and conclude global agreements as a Union.

The effectiveness of the E-Privacy Directive depends on its implementation in national legislation and on the enforcement mechanisms put in place. Member States were quite late with national implementation, however, by now the majority of Member States have adopted transposition measures. While most Member States chose to implement the provisions on spam of the E-Privacy Directive in their data protection laws, other Member States amended their consumer codes, telecommunications codes, their competition laws, or made brand new instruments to fulfill their obligations under EU law.

One thing is clear. Member States have used every discretionary competence they had to provide for their own arrangements under the Directive. Large differences exist between individual Member States in terms of scope of protection they decided to offer users as well as in terms of the position of legal persons.

Other differences will arise, because the Directive leaves the interpretation of a number of relevant aspects to national law, national courts and national regulatory authorities. Furthermore, a number of questions that could arise from new anti-spam law belong to the domain of civil law which is left largely unharmonized within the EU.

In terms of the effectiveness of the new European regime, a lot depends on whether effective enforcement mechanisms are put in place. Effective and timely enforcement is essential to ensure it is for that reason that the European Commission has stressed in its 2004 Communication on spam that Member States should work on effective enforcement and accessible complaint mechanisms. The choice of enforcement methods has been largely left up to individual Member States, which in effect means that very different systems have been put in place. Issues like complaint mechanisms, choice of public of administrative law and penalties are dealt with in altogether different ways. Also, the question of who is to enforce the Directive is answered differently in different countries. In some Member States, like France and the United Kingdom, the Data Protection Commissioner is in charge of enforcement, while in other countries, like the Netherlands this is a responsibility of the National Regulatory Authority. In Sweden, enforcement is left up to the Consumer Protection Authority, the Ombudsman. At this moment, in Germany there is no authority at all to enforce the implemented provisions and enforcement is left up to private parties and, to our opinion, it is questionable whether without public enforcement authority, it could be said that real protection of subscribers is ensured.

To improve effective enforcement of the provisions on spam, co-ordination among the responsible authorities is facilitated and promoted through an informal on-line group and in the context of the CNSA, the 'Contact Network of Spam Authorities'. The recently concluded co-operation protocol has established a common procedure for handling cross-border complaints on spam. While this is a promising development, its effects should not be overestimated. However, nowhere near all of the responsible authorities have joined this agreement, and compliance is voluntary.

Because of the differences in national implementation measures taken, combined with the fact that enforcement is not harmonized at all, the anti-spam framework put into place is rather confusing. There are too many diverges in implementation methods to be effective on a Pan-European Level and a harmonized enforcement framework should be adopted too. In practice, it is to be expected that cross border complaints will be a big obstacle to effective enforcement in the years to come.

We have seen that the legal approach to spam must be complemented with other measures, most notably technological measures and consumer awareness programs. The risks of false positives and false negatives should however not be underestimated and warrant further analysis. Consumer awareness is an important way to protect users but is not the panacea to spam either. Besides the new regulatory approach to spam, consumers and businesses can still use other parts of the law to fight spam. Trespass to chattel can be a ground for providers to refuse spammers access to their networks. Civil law tort could be relevant in some user-spammer cases. In some instances, it could also be viable to address the vendors which use spammers to sell their products.

Furthermore, employers must be made aware of the risk of new computer related liabilities. An important example of a potential new liability is the risk of being held accountable for not sufficiently protecting employees against unsolicited pornographic e-mail. American case law shows that these lawsuits can be a dangerous reality and it is something employers should be aware of. Besides that, liability could arise out of behavior of employees such as for example sending out unsolicited e-mail. Another risk is connected to the technological measures taken against spam. There is always a certain risk that due to false positives good e-mails are not delivered which of course can cause harm. However, an obvious risk posed by spam to companies is without a doubt the loss of productivity and the increased bandwidth cost involved.

A development with serious security implications is the convergence of spam and viruses. The E-Privacy Directive addresses security issues and requires appropriate measures to be taken by providers. This does not introduce a strong right for users to object to their providers about letting through spam. Under certain circumstances, tort law or contract law could oblige providers to take measures against spam and viruses, such as filtering. A duty to act could be reasonable as soon as the access to either network or services is threatened due to spam and viruses. ISP's should inform their customers about their spam policy and possibly about the technological solutions available.

A final remark on this subject must be made. Instead of focusing on legislative solutions, one could also propose the following. If every sender of e-mail would pay a small amount per sent message, it would not be profitable for spammers to spam.

When we focus our attention on getting spammers to stop spamming by legislative means and effective enforcement mechanisms to protect this cheap communication vehicle, we must realize that the legislative process behind the spam measures and enforcement mechanisms are not cheap at all. Although we might not be paying per messages, we are paying trough taxes.

8.2   RECOMMENDATIONS

- The EU should consider additional actions in order to promote effective enforcement mechanisms.

The European Commission should monitor the effects of the E-Privacy Directive closely and focus in particular on the enforcement of Article 13. In our opinion, additional measures are necessary in order to achieve effective enforcement throughout the EU, preferably the adoption of a harmonized enforcement framework.

- Further guidelines should be given as to the correct interpretation of a number of key elements in Article 13.

The correct interpretation of a number of key elements of Article 13 is too important to the fight against spam that a further Communication is needed to give guidance. Especially the continued confusion about Article 13(2) shows the need for a harmonized interpretation.

- Further co-operation between NRA's, Data Protection Authorities and other responsible authorities is desirable.

In order to provide effective enforcement, accessible complaint mechanisms are needed.

The probability of European cross border spam complaints requires the responsible authorities to co-operate. While the adoption of the CNSA co-operation protocol is a promising development, its effects should not be overestimated. In order to be effective, all responsible authorities should join the agreement, and compliance to the agreement should be mandatory. Transparent complaint mechanisms for consumers are needed.

- International co-operation should be intensified.

The success of the EU regulation depends in large part of its practical effect on consumers inboxes. Therefore, the proliferation of third country spam must also be stopped. International co-operation is very important to achieve this. The momentum to tackle the spam problem is definitely there, and more substantial steps to fight spam need to be made. A well-co-ordinated, multilateral international framework is needed.

The European Union should initiate more of a co-operative policy and conclude global agreements as a Union, instead of fostering its Member States to engage in bilateral co-operation.

- Every country should have only one authority dealing with spam.

CNSA should co-ordinate an effort to reduce the number of different national authorities dealing with spam complaints and enforcement of spam regulation. Preferably countries should leave enforcement to the same type authority. Enforcement of spam regulation seems a natural role for National Regulatory Authorities to play.

- Consumer awareness should be promoted at the national level.

It is very important that consumers are aware of the new European rules, of the risks with regard to spam and of the possibilities to stop it. Awareness also includes knowing where to file a complaint. Also, it is important that users know not to opt-out to certain illegitimate spam messages. This is typically a matter that should be directed at the national level.

- The responsibility of users with regard to the security of their computers should be defined at the national level.

Users must be aware of the fact that their computer too could turn into a spam machine if backdoors are left wide open. It is important to stress that everybody has a responsibility in stopping spam.

- Stopping e-mail address harvesting should be an objective.

Making it harder to collect e-mail addresses should be part of a concerted effort to fight spam. DPA's should play a leading role in this effort, co-ordinated by the Article 29 Working Party.

- The development of technological solutions will be important and should be brought to the attention of market players and consumers.

The only solution to spam is a combined effort of legal, educational and technological measures. It is important that users and corporations are aware of the possibilities technology offers but also of the inherent risks of those technologies as false positives and false negatives are likely to happen.

- Businesses should be made aware of the risks spam poses not only in terms of costs and productivity loss but also in terms of possible liabilities.

The offensive nature of some spam messages renders it important to take measures to protect employees against those messages. Also, liability could exist for an employee sending out spam from a company machine.

- ISP's should adopt further measures to protect their customers against spam or at least inform them about the possibilities to fight spam.

The responsibility of ISP's with regard to providing security remain largely undefined. However, as spam and viruses sometimes converge into 'V-spam' ISP's should inform their customers about the related risks and perhaps about the possibilities to protect oneself against spam. The role of the provider in the fight against spam and viruses should be debated at the EU level.

REFERENCES

AOUN AND RASIE 2003
Frederic Aoun and Bruno Rasie, 'Do social applications pose a threat?', available at <http://www.halte-au-spam.com>.

ARTICLE 29 WORKING PARTY 2000A
Article 29 Working Party, Working Document: 'Privacy on the Internet – An integrated EU Approach to On-line Data Protection', adopted 21 November 2000.

ARTICLE 29 WORKING PARTY 2000B
Article 29 Working Party, Opinion 2/2000 concerning the general review of the telecommunications legal framework, adopted 3 February 2000.

ARTICLE 29 WORKING PARTY 2003
Article 29 Working Party, Opinion 3/2003 on the European code of conduct of FEDMA for the use of personal data in direct marketing, adopted 13 June 2003.

ARTICLE 29 WORKING PARTY 2004
Article 29 Working Party, Opinion 5/2004 on unsolicited communications for marketing purposes under Article 13 of Directive 2002/58/EC, adopted 27 February 2004.

BOARDMAN 2004A
Ruth Boardman, 'Direct Marketing – The new rules', *Hertfordshire Law Journal* 2(1), 3-30.

BOARDMAN 2004B
Ruth Boardman, 'E-mail-marketing in the EU-Part III on Italy, The Netherlands and Sweden', available at <http://www.twobirds.com/english/publications/articles/E-mail_marketing_in_the_EUptIII.cfm>.

BOARDMAN 2004C
Ruth Boardman, 'E-mail-marketing in the EU-Part II on Belgium and Germany', available at <http://www.twobirds.com/english/publications/articles/E-mail_marketing_in_the_EUptII.cfm>.

BUTLER 2003
Mike Butler, 'Spam, the meat of the problem', *Computer Law and Security Report,* Vol. 19, No. 5 2003, Elsevier Ltd.

CHARLESWORTH 2003
Andrew Charlesworth, 'Information privacy law in the European Union: e pluribus unum or ex uno plures'?, *Hastings Law Journal,* April 2003.

CHAVANNES 2003
Remy Chavannes, 'Spam: abonnees, ontvangers en de kracht van de bestuurlijke boete' ('Spam: subscribers, recipients and administrative sanctions, unauthorized translation'), *Mediaforum* 2003-11/12, p. 357.

COHEN AND MILLER 2003
Ronnie Cohen and Jamie S. Miller, 'Towards a theory of cyber place: a proposal for a new legal framework', *Richmond Journal of Law & Technology* 2003-10/2.

COMMUNICATION FROM THE COMMISSION TO THE EUROPEAN PARLIAMENT
concerning the common position of the Council on the adoption of the E-Privacy Directive. Communication from the Commission to the European Parliament pursuant to the second subparagraph of Article 251(2) of the EC Treaty concerning the common position of the Council on the adoption of a Directive of the European Parliament and of the Council on processing of personal data and the protection of privacy in the electronic communications sector /*SEC/2002/0124 final – COD 2000/0189*.

COMMUNICATION 2004
Communication from the Commission to the European Parliament, the Council, the European Economic and Social Committee and the Committee of the Regions on unsolicited commercial communications or 'spam', Brussels 22 January 2004, COM (2004) 28 final.

CO-OPERATION PROCEDURE 2004
Co-operation procedure concerning the transmission of complaint information and intelligence relevant to the enforcement of Article 13 of the Privacy and Electronic Communication Directive 2002/58, or any other applicable national law pertaining to the use of unsolicited electronic communications, 1 December 2004.

COUNCIL CONCLUSIONS 2004
Council Conclusions on unsolicited communications for direct marketing purposes or spam, 2 December 2004.

DONOVAN 2004

Colleen Donovan, 'Implementation of the E-Privacy Directive in the UK – Understanding the new rules', *Computer Law & Security Report,* Vol. 20 No. 2 2004, Elsevier Ltd.

EP RECOMMENDATION for a second reading on the common position on the E-Privacy Directive, April 2002. Recommendation for second reading on the common position adopted by the Council with a view to adopting a European Parliament and Council Directive concerning the processing of personal data and the protection of privacy in the electronic communications sector – Committee on Citizens' Freedoms and Rights, Justice and Home Affairs, 22 April 2002, A5-0130/2002.

FEDMA's CODE OF PRACTICE

Federation of European Direct Marketing, European Code of Practice for the use of personal data in direct marketing, available at <http://www.fedma.org/img/db/FEDMACodeEN.pdf>.

FINGER AND SCHMIEDER 2005

M.Finger and S. Schmieder, 'The new law against unfair competition; an assessment', 6 *German LJ* (2005), p. 202, available at <http://www.germanlawjournal.com>.

FISHER 2000

Michael A. Fisher, 'The right to spam? Regulating electronic junk mail', *Columbia VLA Journal of Law & Arts* 363 (2000).

FRITZEMEYER AND LAW 2005

Wolfgang Fritzemeyer and Andrew Law, 'The CAN-SPAM Act – Analysed from a European Perspective', *C.T.L.R.* 2005, 11 (3), pp. 81-90.

FUNK, ZEIFANG, JOHNSON, SPESSAR III 2004

A. Funk, G. Zeifang, D.T. Johnson, R.W. Spessar III, 'Unsolicited Commercial E-mails in the Jurisdictions of Germany and the USA', *Cri* 2004, pp. 138-144.

GAUTHRONET AND DROUARD 2001

Serge Gauthronet and Etienne Drouard, 'Unsolicited Commercial communications and Data Protection', January 2001, available at <http://europa.eu.int/comm/internal_market/privacy/docs/studies/spamstudy_en.pdf>.

GEISLER 2001
R.J. Geisler, 'Whether 'Anti-Spam' Laws Violate The First Amendment', *Journal of Online Law* 2001, Art. 8.

GRAHAM 2002A
Paul Graham, 'Filters vs Blacklists', available at <http://www.paul graham.com/falsepositives.html>.

GRAHAM 2002B
Paul Graham, 'Will filters kill spam?', available at <http://www.paul graham.com/wfks.html>.

GRAHAM 2003
Paul Graham, 'Stopping spam', available at <http://www.paulgraham. com/stopspam.html>.

ICO GUIDANCE 2003
Guidance to the privacy and electronic communications (EC Directive) Regulations 2003. Part 1: Marketing by Electronic Means, issued by the Information Commissioner's Office in November 2003.

9th IMPLEMENTATION REPORT
9th Report on the Implementation of the Telecommunications Regulatory Package, COM(2003) 715 final.

10th IMPLEMENTATION REPORT
European Electronic Communications Regulation and Markets 2004 (10th Report), COM(2004) 759 final.

ITU TASK FORCE ON SPAM TOOLKIT 2005
Task Force on Spam, Outline for the OECD Anti-spam toolkit (work plan), 11 May 2005, JT00184012, prepared by the Directorate for Science, Technology and Industry, Committee on Consumer Policy and the Committee for Information, Computer and Communications Policy.

KABEL 2003A
Jan Kabel, 'Spam: A Terminal Threat to ISPs? The legal position of ISPs concerning their Anti-Spam Policies in the EU after the Privacy & Telecom Directive', *Computer Law Review International* 2003-1, pp. 6-10.

KABEL 2003B
Jan Kabel, 'Swings on the Horizontal. The search for Consistency in European Advertising law', *Iris Plus* 2003-8, pp. 2-8. Available at <http://www.ivir.nl/publications/kabel/swings.pdf>.

KABEL 2002
Jan Kabel, 'Reclamerecht online, problemen in theorie en praktijk' (advertisement law online, problems in theory and practice, unauthorized translation), available at <http://www.ivir.nl/publicaties/kabel/reclamerecht_online.pdf>.

KABEL 2000A
Jan Kabel, 'Commercial communications', in: *Study on Consumer Law and the Information Society*, Amsterdam: PriceWaterHouseCoopers (2000), pp. 22-38.

KABEL 2000B
Jan Kabel, 'Commerciële uitingen' (Commercial expression, unauthorized translation), in F. Grosheide (red.), *Hoofdstukken Communicatie & Mediarecht*, Nijmegen: Ars Aequi Libri 2000, pp. 269-270.

KABEL 2000C
Jan Kabel, 'Analysis of the existing European Law on the commercial communications in the light of the new conditions created by the Information Society', in: *Study on Consumer Law and the Information Society*, Amsterdam: PriceWaterHouseCoopers (2000), pp. 1-15.

KAM 2004
Steven Kam, 'Trespass to Chattels and the Doctrine of Cyber-nuisance', 19 *Berkeley Technology Law Journal* 427 (2004).

KELIN 2001
Sabra-Anne Kelin, 'State Regulation of unsolicited commercial e-mail', *Berkeley Technology Law Journal* 2001, p. 435.

KHONG 2000
Wye-Keen Khong, Regulating spam on the internet, 15th BILETA Conference: 'Electronic datasets and access to legal information', 14 April 2000. Available at <http://www.bileta.ac.uk/00papers/khong.html>.

KUILWIJK 2000
Kees Jan Kuilwijk, 'Recent developments in E.U. privacy protection regulation', *International trade law and regulation* 2000, 6(6), pp. 200-206.

LODDER 2004
A.R. Lodder, *Spam, Spammer ,... Analyse van het recht en de techniek rond elektronische ongevraagde commerciële communicatie, in het bijzonder via e-mail,* Den Haag: SDU Uitgevers, 2004.

MAGEE 2003
John Magee, 'The law regulating unsolicited commercial e-mail: An international perspective', *19 Santa Clara Computer & High Technology Law Journal* 333, May 2003.

MESSAGELABS INTELLIGENCE REPORT 2005
MessageLabs Intelligence: June 2005, available at <www.messagelabs.com>.

OECD 2004
OECD, Directorate for science, technology and industry, Committee for information, computer and communications policy, 'background paper for the OECD workshop on spam', DSTI/ICCP(2003)10/FINAL, 22 January 2004, available at <www.oecd.org>.

OECD 2005
OECD, Directorate for science, technology and industry, committee for information, computer and communications policy, Task Force on Spam, 'Anti-spam Law Enforcement Report', DSTI/CP/ICCP/SPAM(2004)3/FINAL, 13 May 2005, available at <www.oecd.org>.

OPINION OF THE COMMISSION amending the proposal for the E-Privacy Directive, June 2002. Opinion of the Commission pursuant to Article 251(2), third subparagraph, point (c) of the EC Treaty, on the European Parliament's amendments to the Council's common position regarding the proposal for a Directive of the European Parliament and of the Council on the processing of personal data and the protection of privacy in the electronic communications sector amending the proposal of the commission pursuant to Article 250(2) of the EC Treaty, 17 June 2002, COM(2002) 338 final.

OWEN AND KIERNAN EARL 2003
Mark Owen and Elizabeth Kiernan Earl, 'Data Protection the European Way: a discussion of the legislative framework adopted in the European Union', *Sedona Conference Journal Fall* 2003.

PENVEN AND WILHELM 2004
A. Penven and P. Wilhelm, 'Prospection commerciale par courrier électronique: le nouvel article L. 121-20-5 du code de la consommation', *Legipresse* No. 215, Octobre 2004, pp. 105-109.

PRESIDENCY PAPER 2004
Presidency paper on unsolicited communications for direct marketing purposes or spam, 24 November 2004.

PROPOSAL FOR THE E-PRIVACY DIRECTIVE 2000
Proposal for a Directive of the European Parliament and of the Council concerning the processing of personal data and the protection of privacy in the electronic communications, 12 July 2000, COM (2000) 385 final.

REPORT ON THE PROPOSAL FOR THE E-PRIVACY DIRECTIVE 2001, JULY 2001
Report on the proposal for a European Parliament and Council Directive concerning the processing of personal data and the protection of privacy in the electronic communications sector – Committee on Citizens' Freedoms and Rights, Justice and Home Affairs, 13 July 2001, FINAL A5-0270/2001.

REPORT OF THE WORKING GROUP ON INTERNET GOVERNANCE 2005
Report of the Working Group on Internet Governance, June 2005, available at <http://www.wgig.org/docs/WGIGREPORT.pdf>.

ROJINSKY AND TEISSONNIERE 2005
C. Rojinsky and G. Teissonniere, 'L'encadrement du commerce électronique par la loi française du 21 juin 2004 pour la confiance dans l'economie numérique', *Lex Electronica,* Vol. 10, No 1, Hiver 2005 <http://www.lex-electronica.org/articles/v10-1/rojinsky_teissonniere.htm>.

SCHAUB 2002
M.Y. Schaub, 'Unsolicited e-mail, does Europe allow spam? The state of the art of the European legislation with regard to unsolicited commercial communications', *Computer Law & Security Report* Vol. 18 No. 2, 2002, pp. 99-105.

SCHIEFELBINE 2003
Erich D. Schiefelbine, 'Stopping a Trojan Horse: challenging pop-up advertisements and embedded software schemes on the internet through unfair competition laws', *Santa Clara Computer and High Technology Law Journal,* May 2003.

SIEBECKER 2003
Michael R. Siebecker, 'Cookies and the common law: are internet advertisers trespassing at our computers?', *Southern California Law Review,* May 2003, p. 893.

SOLA POOL, DE
I. de Sola Pool, *Technologies of Freedom*, Cambridge (MA): Harvard University Press, 1983.

SORKIN 2001
David E. Sorkin, 'Technical and Legal Approaches to Unsolicited Electronic Mail', 35 *U.S.F. Law Review* 325-2001, pp. 325-384.

THOLE 2003
E. Thole, *SPAM from the European Union Perspective*, Report to the CLA Munich Conference, 13-14 November, 2003.

THOLE 2004
E. Thole, 'De E-Privacy richtlijn maakt geen einde aan spam', *NJB* 2004, pp. 168-173.

TRZASKOWSKI 2003
Jan Trzaskowski, 'Cross-Border Law Enforcement in the Information Society', available at <http://www.legalriskmanagement.artscape.dk/uploads/Artikler/Julebog2003.pdf>.

1985 RECOMMENDATION OF THE COUNCIL OF EUROPE on the protection of personal data used for the purposes of direct marketing. Recommendation No. R (85) 20 of the Committee of Ministers to Member States on the protection of personal data used for the purposes of Direct Marketing (Adopted by the Committee of Ministers on 24 October 1985 at the 389th meeting of the Ministers' Deputies, available at <http://www.coe.int>.

WSIS DECLARATION OF PRINCIPLES 2003
WSIS Declaration of Principles: Building the Information Society: a global challenge in the new millennium, 12 December 2003, DOC WSIS-03/GENEVA/DOC/4-E.

WSIS ACTION PLAN 2003
WSIS Action Plan, 12 December 2003, DOC WSIS-03/GENEVA/DOC/5-E.

INFORMATION TECHNOLOGY & LAW SERIES

1. E-Government and its Implications for Administrative Law – Regulatory Initiatives in France, Germany, Norway and the United States (The Hague: T·M·C·ASSER PRESS, 2002)
   Editor: J.E.J. Prins / ISBN 90-6704-141-6
2. Digital Anonymity and the Law – Tensions and Dimensions (The Hague: T·M·C·ASSER PRESS, 2003)
   Editors: C. Nicoll, J.E.J. Prins and M.J.M. van Dellen /
   ISBN 90-6704-156-4
3. Protecting the Virtual Commons – Self-Organizing Open Source and Free Software Communities and Innovative Intellectual Property Regimes (The Hague: T·M·C·ASSER PRESS, 2003)
   Authors: R. van Wendel de Joode, J.A. de Bruijn and M.J.G. van Eeten /
   ISBN 90-6704-159-9
4. IT Support and the Judiciary – Australia, Singapore, Venezuela, Norway, The Netherlands and Italy (The Hague: T·M·C·ASSER PRESS, 2004)
   Editors: A. Oskamp, A.R. Lodder and M. Apistola /
   ISBN 90-6704-168-8
5. Electronic Signatures – Authentication Technology from a Legal Perspective (The Hague: T·M·C·ASSER PRESS, 2004)
   Author: M.H.M. Schellekens / ISBN 90-6704-174-2
6. Virtual Arguments – On the Design of Argument Assistants for Lawyers and Other Arguers (The Hague: T·M·C·ASSER PRESS, 2004)
   Author: B. Verheij / ISBN 90-6704-190-4
7. Reasonable Expectations of Privacy? – Eleven Country Reports on Camera Surveillance and Workplace Privacy (The Hague: T·M·C·ASSER PRESS, 2005)
   Editors: S. Nouwt, B.R. de Vries and J.E.J. Prins / ISBN 90-6704-198-X
8. Unravelling the Myth Around Open Source Licences – An Analysis from a Dutch and European Law Perspective (The Hague: T·M·C·ASSER PRESS, 2006)
   Authors: L. Guibault and O. van Daalen / ISBN 90-6704-214-5
9. Starting Points for ICT Regulation – Deconstructing Prevalent Policy One-Liners (The Hague: T·M·C·ASSER PRESS, 2006)
   Editors: B-J. Koops, M. Lips, J.E.J. Prins and M. Schellekens /
   ISBN 90-6704-216-1
10. Regulating Spam – A European Perspective after the Adoption of the E-Privacy Directive (The Hague: T·M·C·ASSER PRESS, 2006)
    Authors: L.F. Asscher and S.A. Hoogcarspel / ISBN 90-6704-220-X

GPSR Compliance
The European Union's (EU) General Product Safety Regulation (GPSR) is a set
of rules that requires consumer products to be safe and our obligations to
ensure this.

If you have any concerns about our products, you can contact us on

ProductSafety@springernature.com

In case Publisher is established outside the EU, the EU authorized
representative is:

Springer Nature Customer Service Center GmbH
Europaplatz 3
69115 Heidelberg, Germany

www.ingramcontent.com/pod-product-compliance
Lightning Source LLC
LaVergne TN
LVHW050151060326
832904LV00003B/118

9 789067 042208